Whuzup With the Hood;

The inner city's state, source & solution

RICHARD D. SIEMS

Whuzup With the Hood

CONTENTS

PART ONE: THE WAY IT IS
Welcome to the Inner City

Deep within the ever-growing mass of humanity in any large American city is a culture unknown to most and misunderstood by many. It is hated by some and feared by others. It has been tagged with labels such as "the slums," "the ghetto," and "the hood." Each of these produces a mental image that is rarely accurate. Though frequently considered an anti-culture it is really an emerging culture.

The inner city is a culture so unique that it is as hard to describe as it is to understand. By some measures it is a micro society regressing toward chaos. By other measures it is a developing society that is influencing all of America. And, it is growing.

I have been involved in inner city America for more than a decade. Some will wonder how anyone can profess to have learned much in such a short time. It is a comparatively short time. However, it has been long enough to observe much, analyze a lot, and understand at least some. I do not, nor will I ever, know the inner city as intimately as second or third generation urban-dwellers. However, with newness comes objectivity.

Serving in the inner city has been an incredible journey for me. I am a second career guy. After over twenty-five years of progression as an engineer, engineering manager, and executive mostly in the chemical processing industry, I was burdened to make a difference socially and spiritually. I did not purpose to work in the inner city; but rather just landed there. Having been raised in the world's finest middle class home, I was saddened at times, scared at times, and shocked at times. Yet, I am energized by the relationships I've enjoyed there.

Previous foreign travel experience partially prepared me for my urban experience. I had learned to accept other's customs and learned enough of their language to get by. The inner city is indeed foreign to most of us. This book is not a travel log of my urban voyage but includes some of my personal experiences as illustrations. This is my description of the inner city, how urban impoverished residents live, what causes the environment in which they live, how and why it affects us all, and what it will take to improve that environment.

It is important to note that not everyone in the inner city fits the following description. At times as you read you may think everything about the inner city is bad. It isn't. There are good homes, strong families, well-educated residents, reliable institutions, good businesses, convenient transportation systems, great employees and wonderful people. Unfortunately, these are not a majority.

You honor me by reading this book. I commit to help you understand and I aspire to move you to action.

THE FACE - The Urban Setting & the Urban Lifestyle (Chapter one)

What is your neighborhood like? What are its social, economic, physical, and spiritual characteristics? How do you picture an inner city neighborhood? Pause for a moment to focus your mental image of the inner city. I presupposed the state of the inner city before I became involved. My image was very inaccurate. I correctly anticipated some characteristics but others really surprised me!

Some aspects of the inner city are best described with facts and statistics. From extensive research I have determined that facts and statistics are 93.3 percent boring. They are, however, necessary to describe the inner city. I assure you that if you hate facts and stats, the other chapters have very few.

Looking at the characteristics of the inner city is like looking at someone's face. The person inside is partly obvious as visible clues project outward. So are cities.

There are as many different inner city faces as there are urban areas in America. For anyone to believe that they understand them all would be naïve, and for me to imply that I can describe them all would be absurd. Like human faces, the faces of the inner city have some common characteristics. We can better understand a whole by examining one characteristic at a time. Here, look carefully at the typical inner city's face.

Size or Scope

The size of any single inner city and the breadth of the national urban-impoverished society are much debated. Several varied descriptions of the hood have been expressed;

there are as many descriptions as there are analysts. A major characteristic of any inner city is poverty. Poverty measures can be used to indicate the cumulative size of American inner cities. As you would expect, there are different definitions of poverty. A subset of them is shown later in this chapter in the Income section. I think that an order-of-magnitude scope is sufficient for now.

The 2010 US Census Bureau classifies 11.3% of American <u>families</u> living below the poverty level. (1/ US Census Bureau) That means that 8,598,062 of the total 76,089,045 families in this country live in poverty. (1/ US Census Bureau) The percent of American <u>individuals</u> below the poverty level is even higher, because families in poverty are larger than the average American family. At 15.3% of the US population or 46,215,956 persons. (2/ US Census Bureau) It is interesting to further note that nearly half of these individuals, 20,413,453, live below 50% of the poverty level. (2/ US Census Bureau)

Not all impoverished families live in the inner city but a large portion do. No data listing that portion were found, so I estimated it. Unable to find similar data in the U.S. 2010 Census, I used the U.S. 2000 Census which identifies 31.1% of Americans as living in "central city" and 8.8% living "rural." (3/ US Census Bureau) Since these are the two areas where the impoverished live, I am assuming a similar distribution of people in poverty. Thus, it appears that about three-fourths of the impoverished, 34,661,967 people, live in inner cities.

The growth rate of poverty changes through time. According to the US Census Bureau the percent of total US population living in poverty increased in the 1970s and 1980s but decreased slightly in the 1990s. (4/ Proctor & Dalaker, page 22) The number of impoverished Americans fluctuates with the economy, employment, social program effectiveness, and the definition of poverty level. US Census information shows that the number in poverty has again been steadily increasing since the year 2000. In fact, it had increased from 12.4% to 12.7% of the total population in 2004. (5/ US Census Bureau) Thus, in four years nearly 1,000,000 people had joined those already impoverished. Since then the growth rate has accelerated such that over 11,000,000 people were added to those below the poverty line, most of them since the housing bubble burst in 2007.

Throughout this book three names are used for the subject area – inner city, inner-urban, and the hood. Readers may incorrectly assume the hood refers only to African-American neighborhoods. In this book it is used to mean any area where urban impoverished live irrespective of national origin. Inner-city dwellers, inner-urban dwellers, poor urbanites, those in the hood, and the urban impoverished refer to those who live there. I use these names as synonyms solely for variety. Please accept them for the duration of this book.

Ethnicity

People from most ethnic backgrounds are present in the hood. U.S. 2010 Census data doesn't identify the ethnic makeup of the inner city. It does, however, list the ethnic background of those in poverty. African Americans, Native Americans and Hispanics or Latinos are twice as likely to live in poverty as Caucasians or Asians. The listed percentages are 27.1% of African Americans, 28.4% of Native Americans, 24.8% of Hispanics, 12.5% of Caucasians and 12.5% of Asians have incomes below the poverty line. (2/ US Census Bureau) My experience confirms that the majority of inner-urban dwellers are African American, Native American and Hispanic.

Homes and Housing

Some cities have large concentrated inner-urban areas while others have numerous small dispersed areas. Some inner city areas are contiguous blocks of high-rise buildings. Others are mostly small apartment houses, eight-plexes, four-plexes and duplexes.

Most poor urbanites rent their living spaces. According to 2010 US Census data 68.8% of Americans live in homes that they own. (6/ US Census Bureau) I found no data listing the percentage of homes owned by those below the poverty line. I assume it is very small since 84.7% of Americans have incomes above the poverty line and 68.8% of Americans own the home in which they live. My experience supports that assumption because I have met very few inner city occupant home owners.

Inner-city dwellers live in neighborhoods that were formerly occupied by middle class families who with more means moved out to the suburbs. They left behind well-established but declining neighborhoods. Those same neighborhoods are now blighted with abandoned buildings and over-priced, over-worn apartments and homes. Many need major repair, renovation, or even replacement. Appliances are generally old and in poor condition. Occasionally the furnace or water heater has failed. Bathrooms are frequently in disrepair and occasionally out of service. Floors and walls routinely have cracks and holes that allow insects and rodents easy ingress. Such holes escalate already high utility costs in poorly insulated buildings.

Many of the residents of these marginal dwellings do not have steady income so they frequently struggle with utility shut-offs. Hence, they are transient, constantly moving to a different apartment to restart utilities. It is not unusual for a tenant or a landlord to become so frustrated that the renter leaves or is evicted. Far too frequently residents live through a northern winter without heat or a southern summer without air conditioning. Some do not even have running water. When available funds will not cover all the expenses, many choose food and medicine over comfort and hygiene. I have visited many homes that have exterior doors that will not lock, rags stuffed in the holes in broken windowpanes, bugs and rodents, and no utilities.

The typical home is disorderly and disorganized with clutter everywhere. Discarded items like news-papers, magazines, and empty food containers are piled in corners. Important items may have been misplaced.

Pets are highly valued. Some homes have many cats or dogs. Pet hair and feces are obvious in these homes. I have visited homes with as many as a dozen cats or four dogs inside. It is noteworthy that in the inner city cats and dogs have more than "pet value." They are often protection from rodents and ill-intentioned people.

Family Unit

Inner-urban family life is unlike most of America. Few families live together as father, mother, and children. Most children live with only one parent, normally the mother. Some are in the care of a grandmother or an aunt or an older sibling. A large number of children never see their fathers, many of which are incarcerated or have abandoned them. Some children do not know their father and may not even know his name. Urban-impoverished women commonly have more children than their counterparts. Such conditions contribute to poverty and dysfunction. Indianapolis Juvenile Court Judge Marilyn Moore proclaimed that the "kids who are seen in court are increasingly damaged. A major cause is that unskilled parents are raising too many kids. Kids are having kids."

An extreme example is Vonnette (Vonnette is a real person but like the others cited in this book, her name has been changed to respect privacy) who has thirteen children from seven different fathers. She and her children live in a small, shabby apartment with Vonnette's current live-in. Though Vonnette has more kids than the average urban impoverished mother, single mothers with many children by several fathers is common.

Occasionally both parents are incarcerated or unwilling to care for their offspring. I salute the grandmothers, aunts, and other family and friends that care for such inner city children. These care-givers are pillars holding up the remnants of a rapidly crumbling family structure.

Family is a major determinant in child development. According to *Experiments in Living: The Fatherless Family* by Rebecca O'Neill, (7/ O'Neill)
- 63% of all youth suicides are from fatherless homes
- 90% of all homeless and runaway children are from fatherless homes
- 85% of all children that exhibit behavioral disorders come from fatherless homes
- 80% of rapists motivated with displaced anger come from fatherless homes
- 71% of all high school dropouts come from fatherless homes
- 70% of juveniles in state operated institutions come from fatherless homes
- 85% of all youths sitting in prisons grew up in a fatherless home

Wow! It's quite obvious that since urban families rarely have a father in the home, the children have are predisposed to societal dysfunction.

There are exceptions. Some families are strong and productive families who could, but choose not to, live elsewhere. I celebrate them! They choose to be part of the solution, not part of the problem. Unfortunately they are an anomaly. Many more are needed to roll up their sleeves and dig in to help others!

Relationships are very important. When the only available help comes from other people, the people who help are highly valued. In that way family is very important to inner-urban dwellers. Extended families frequently gather to enjoy food or entertainment.

Safety & Security

It should be no surprise that inner-city dwellers are not as safe or secure as residents of other communities. Abundant printed matter expounds the correlation between poverty, overcrowding, lack of literacy, and crime.

The inner-urban incident rates for most crimes are many times those in other segments of the community. No data segregating inner city crime rates were found. The FBI lists violent crime rates for Metropolitan Areas as being about two and a half times those of nonmetropolitan areas. (8/ US Department of Justice) Experience shows that a major portion of metropolitan violent crime occurs in the hood. National crime rates have recently fallen. (9/ Gallup) Hence, the disparity between the national average and inner city violent crime rate is widening. The conditions in the inner city foster crime. Urban impoverished children are raised in the midst of substance abuse and deviant, criminal behavior. Those conditions increase the likelihood that they will also abuse drugs and commit criminal acts.

Many homes have a weapon for protection; usually it is a handgun. Inner-urban dwellers are fond of large intimidating dogs. It appears true that someone with a big dog can get by with a small gun!

Within my first few months working in the inner city I met a man named Joe. I perceived that Joe was mild mannered. After a brief meeting, one of my cohorts asked if Joe had told me his background. I replied no, so he told me about Joe. Joe had just been paroled from the state penitentiary after serving sixteen years for conviction on four counts of second-degree murder. In a later meeting Joe explained to me that when he was in his teens he was riding in a car with four friends. One of them accused Joe of never paying for a drug he had purchased. A struggle ensued inside the car. One of the four threw a white powder in his face blurring his vision. Joe instinctively reached for his piece and began randomly shooting. When the ordeal was over, the other four were mortally wounded. Within hours Joe was arrested, charged and incarcerated then later tried, convicted and imprisoned.

Inner city crime is really terrorism! It's not generally referred to as such, but it is. The thuggery in inner-urban areas is really no different from what is happening in corrupt foreign countries. It disappoints me that this violence has not been called terrorism; likely because it is from within rather than from the outside. Our neighbors are killing each other. That does not make it any less terroristic. A few are terrorizing many. We do not allow such behavior from outsiders, so why do we condone it from insiders?

Education

Countless research projects have been completed and reports written describing the condition of inner-urban schools. One that speaks volumes is *Race, Social Class, and Educational Reform in an Inner-city School* by Jean Anyon.

She highlights the seriousness of the situation. In her conclusion she writes "Given the historical correlation between poverty and school failure; given the resiliency of lived professional cultures such as that of school personnel described in this study; and acknowledging the power of the social and cultural differences between racially/economically marginalized school populations and the educational 'help' they receive, it is unlikely that educators in ghetto schools will be successful in making substantial, long term changes in their schools. Thus, I think the only solution to educational resignation and failure in the inner city is the ultimate elimination of poverty and racial degradation. The solution to educational failure in the ghetto is elimination of the ghetto." (10/ Anyon page 89)

Ms. Anyon provides a very strong description. There are infrequent "shining star" inner city schools but most are substandard. Any successful inner-urban school deserves to be modeled and copied.

Education has low priority to the urban impoverished because they perceive no immediate impact on their ability to survive. Data comparing the graduation rates for inner city high schools to the national average could not be located. However, the National Center for Education Statistics (NCES) states that the National Public High School graduation rate for 2008 was 89.9%. (11/ National Center for Education Statistics) Not all graduated in four years. Another NCES report explains that 75.5% of the 2008 class graduated in four years. (12/ National Center for Education Statistics, page 80) Yet another NCES report expresses that the drop-out rate for schools in low income areas is about four times that in affluent areas. (13/ National Center for Education Statistics) Graduation rates for large metropolitan areas are typically lower than for suburban areas. It will be redundant to state that inner cities are surrounded by and therefore a part of large metropolitan areas. USA Today listed the graduation rates within the fifty largest school districts, those in large metro areas. Fourteen of the fifty had graduation rates lower than 50% and three were below 40%! (14/ USA Today)

Inner city graduation rates are characteristically lower than average for the metropolitan area in which they are included. It is not uncommon for inner city graduation rates to be incredibly low. There are some such schools in which only about 30% graduate. The other 70% drop out, are thrown out, are incarcerated, are victims of homicides, or take their own lives. The link between poor education and poverty is well known. The link between poverty and poor education is not as well known but equally evident.

Businesses and Services

Many ordinary service businesses are scarce or totally absent from these inner-urban neighborhoods. I was not surprised by their absence but I was surprised at how this impacts the residents.

Routinely absent are banks and grocery stores. It is commonly believed that banks and grocery stores would not be profitable in these areas because per-capita income is low. However, the concentration of people is higher than in any other area of the city such that there is sufficient financial base to support such enterprises. So why aren't banks and grocery stores located there? Because they are not willing to battle the inherent security concerns. Also, inner-city dwellers are not prone to long-range thinking or planning. They are consumed with the present, getting through today. That focus results in them having no interest in savings accounts or purchasing groceries in large quantities to get better pricing. Often they are not

14

even aware of such options and their advantages.

Most legal inner-urban businesses are convenience stores, gas stations, fast-food restaurants, furniture and appliance rentals, Laundromats, bars, liquor stores, and used car lots.

Transportation

Few inner-urban dwellers own reliable transportation. If they are fortunate (or unfortunate) enough to own an automobile, it needs constant repair. Most residents do not have a sufficient credit rating to purchase a good used car from a reputable dealer. Few buyers know how to identify a good used car. They do not know the common indicators of serviceable versus non-serviceable vehicles so they often purchase maintenance money-pit vehicles. Few have developed auto-mechanic skills so they are easy prey to over-zealous repair shops. They purchase over-used vehicles at buy here, pay here dealers. Such dealers charge very high interest rates. Each state has an interest rate cap for such loans. In most states the maximum interest rate dealers can charge is about the same as it is for credit cards, up to 30%. (15/ Buy Here Pay Here)

Some who drive have no driver's license and most have no auto insurance. When poor driving skills or substance-impaired judgment result in an accident, vehicle repair costs are not reimbursed. Few cities or states have sufficient methods to prevent illegal and uninsured driving. Most cities either have loopholes that allow such practices or do not have enough officers to enforce the laws.

For the urban poor the main transportation modes are walking, riding public transportation, and accompanying a friend in his or her car. Walking is good exercise but many of the places they need to go are too distant from their homes. Most metropolitan areas provide reliable and inexpensive public transportation. A frequent problem is that employment opportunities are distant and during night hours or on weekends. Public transportation often does not operate to those areas at night or on weekends.

We became acutely aware of the lack of transportation in inner New Orleans in 2005 after hurricane Katrina struck the city. A few residents who could have evacuated refused to, but most that stayed in the heavily damaged inner city were the urban-impoverished. They had no transportation or money to acquire transportation. They were stuck in the storm-lashed city.

Employment

Jobs are readily available in the inner city but most pay unlivable wages. Most of the industrial jobs that once served as entry-level work disappeared in the 1990s. Since turnover is very high, additional workers are constantly needed at urban convenience stores, gas stations, fast-food restaurants, Laundromats, bars, liquor stores, and used car lots. Training for these jobs is generally brief and task specific. It is uncommon for an inner-urban worker to keep employment for more than a few weeks or often a few days. Job holding skills are foreign. Quality role models are scarce. Inner city residents may not know anyone who goes to work on every scheduled day or who always arrives on time or who does more than is required of them. These practices are obvious to middle-class workers because they are based on middle-class values.

Direction and criticism are not received well. The urban-impoverished have a general distrust of authority. Personal emergencies constantly interrupt their lives and interfere with attendance and punctuality. Examples of emergencies are a suddenly ill or injured child, utility cut-off, eviction, stolen car, or lost cell phone. They are unable to gauge their own performance. Amount of effort is more important to them than the product of that effort.

For a few years I managed three very small inner city businesses. One was a wholesaler of clothing accessories, the second was an over-flow repackaging business and the third a lawn-care contractor. Each business had similar goals: to temporarily employ impoverished urban residents and teach them the habits necessary to get and keep permanent employment. Supervisory patience and flexibility were imperative as we dealt with the employee issue of the day.

The major issues were,
a) Poor attendance and punctuality. Though desperate for income, they considered neither being at work every day or being on time as important.
b) Lack of initiative. Workers were not accustomed to staying busy during scheduled work time. Their work pace depended on their current mood. Breaks were frequent, arbitrary, and lengthy.
c) Inattention to procedures and details. They were attentive enough to repeat key instructions after having them explained and demonstrated. Most expressed eagerness to comply, but their actions were random and unstructured. Quality work was a foreign concept.
d) Uncontrolled emotions. Employees did not receive direction and correction well. I was at times the target of a verbal tirade. Occasionally I was physically threatened though never assaulted. After such an outburst an employee would just disappear, leave and never return.
e) Mistreatment of tools and equipment. Tools were misused. Equipment was operated without regard for the state of repair or good maintenance techniques. The signs of pending trouble were not recognized or were unheeded and

unreported. Disrepair of equipment and missing or broken tools were frequent and costly to rectify.

Income

The jobs available to inner-city residents are entry-level positions at convenience stores, gas stations, fast-food restaurants, Laundromats, bars, liquor stores, and used car lots. These jobs are normally part-time and rarely provide any fringe benefits. The wages for such jobs are minimum wage. The Federal minimum wage in 2012 is $7.25 per hour. (16/ US Department of Labor) Individual states can set a higher minimum wage. As of June 2012 seventeen states plus the District of Columbia have done so. Those states are Alaska, Arizona, California, Colorado, Connecticut, Florida, Illinois, Maine, Massachusetts, Michigan, Montana, New Mexico, Ohio, Oregon, Rhode Island, Vermont, and Washington. The minimum wage in these states rages from a low of $7.40 in Michigan to a high of $9.04 per hour in Washington. The simple average for all fifty states plus the District of Columbia is $7.49 per hour. (17/ Labor Law Center) Most people cannot survive on such low wages.

According to the United States Department of Commerce the 2010 median household income was $51,914. (18/ US Department of Commerce) The average annual income in the typical American inner city is not readily available. It should suffice to say that most inner-urban residents live far below the poverty level. There is much controversy about poverty in America, at what income the poverty level should be placed, and what factors determine real poverty. The poverty level is not one number but rather a chart of values depending on number of children, number of adults, and ages of those in the home. An order of magnitude mean poverty level annual income for

2010, the most recent available year, would be about $23,000. (19/ Department of Health and Human Services) Very few inner-city residents have incomes nearly this high! For emphasis I repeat, very few urban impoverished families annually earn as much as $23,000.

The US Census Bureau has an additional measure, FCSUM. FCSUM is short for food, clothing, shelter, utilities and medical care. Its value is the average cost of these items. All of these are absolutely necessary. The FCSUM value is also a chart of values graduated by number of family members and their life-stage, not one number. As an example, a reference family with two adults and two kids spent $29,397 for FCSUM in year 2010. (20/ National Academy of Sciences) Most urban-impoverished residents have incomes far below this amount.

Using the FCSUM we can calculate the hourly wage an urban-impoverished worker must earn just to keep up with what we identify in America as absolutely necessary, FCSUM. Few poor urban residents work fulltime. Assume that the average worker works thirty hours per week. In order to receive an annual income of $29,397 their hourly rate must be at least $25.25. If they were fortunate enough to work forty hours per week, they could survive at the FCSUM level on an hourly pay rate of $18.94. It should be obvious that multiple wage earners in a family decreases the hourly rate each earner needs, e.g. two wage earners averaging $12.63 per hour each for thirty hours per week or averaging $9.47 per hour each for forty hours per week can receive $29,397 annually. Compare that to the minimum wage rates listed above: from $7.25 to $9.04 per hour. It will not stretch far enough!

No data were found comparing the unemployment rate or underemployment among urban impoverished to the national average. It may not exist; unemployment numbers include those who try but cannot find employment. After several rejections many inner city residents stop trying.

Finances

Those who do find dependable employment and keep it long enough to get paid by check have fewer financial options than their suburban counterparts. Most are unable to acquire the credit rating required for a checking account or credit card so they make all transactions in cash. They must either find transportation to a bank so they can cash their check for a reasonable fee or cash their check at a walk-to check cashing service. According to the Consumer Federation of America these services routinely charge 2% to 4% fees for paycheck cashing. (21/ Consumer Federation of America) Most of these services make a nice profit from check cashing but their preferred service is short-term loans. They offer one or two week advance loans against a paycheck for anywhere from 390% to 780% APR! (21/ Consumer Federation of America) These short-term loans are packaged to be very enticing to cash-strapped residents with bad credit and few options!

Checking and savings accounts are rare because the institution's locations are inconvenient, most residents cannot clear the credit hurdle, and most lack knowledge of various account types and their relative advantages. So income is low and their net cash amount is even lower.

Food and Provisions

Once income is converted to cash, necessities are purchased. To buy food they can ride the bus for several blocks to the nearest grocery store, buy their food for inflated prices at the convenience store within walking distance, or purchase prepared meals at nearby fast-food restaurants. Convenience food and fast food are more expensive and frequently less healthy than grocery stores.

As with many other subjects, I was unable to find reliable data comparing the average meal cost for food from various sources. However, a review of Internet accessible articles about the difference in the cost of purchasing groceries at a convenience store rather than a grocery store revealed increases from a low of 30% to a high of 100%. I likewise found several Internet articles comparing the average meal cost for fast food versus home cooking. The apparent experience is that typically fast food costs about twice that for meals prepared at home with grocery store acquired food.

Anyone aware of the news in the early twenty-first Century knows of the nutritional issues with fast food and convenience foods. The media blitz must have peaked shortly after the movie *Super Size Me* was released in 2004. Fast food vendors now offer more nutritious options than they did in 2004 but it is widely accepted that the nutrition of fast foods and convenience foods is inferior to well-planned, home-cooked meals.

The inner city business and service impact that surprised me is: inner-urban dwellers start with lower pay (strike one), pay higher conversion fees to cash checks at check cashing establishments (strike two), and pay higher prices for food at convenience stores and fast food restaurants (strike three; they're out!).

Hunger is a major felt-need for those in poverty. AlterNet determined that in 2004 35% of Americans had to choose between food and rent, while 28% had to choose between medical care and food. (22/ Mittal) Some prefer to be housed and medicated rather than full and satisfied.

Elementary aged Jimmy had a parent in prison and was left home alone for most of the week. He qualified for free school breakfast and lunch but did not know where to get an evening meal. Hunger was his weekend companion, as he normally had nothing to eat from Friday noon to Monday morning! Thousands of children share Jimmy's hunger pains every weekend.

Health & Well-being

Inner city populations include inordinately high concentrations of people who experience poor health. Poor health tracks with substance abuse, violence, chronic mental illness, disability, and sexually transmitted diseases such as HIV. These health risks are all over-represented in inner-urban environments. Environmental and social conditions such as high population density, air pollution, social isolation, crime, environmental hazards, and occupational hazards cause or exacerbate illness. Substandard housing, poor nutrition, inadequate food storage and preparation techniques, under-education, high unemployment, and stress often increase health risks.

Health and well-being track with nutrition. Inner-urban nutrition is often substandard because of the lack of quality fresh produce, inadequate kitchen facilities, and limited nutrition education. Knowledge of good nutrition is not innate; it must be acquired.

Though poor-urbanites are more prone to illness, they have access to fewer healthcare options. Most do not have adequate, if any, health insurance. So, some medical procedures are not available to them. Interpreting the 2004 Census Bureau data it is apparent that most other Americans are about twice as likely to have health insurance as inner-city residents. (21/ US Census Bureau)

That may change as the controversial Patient Protection and Affordable Care Act of 2010 (PPACA), informally called Obamacare, is further implemented. Some states provide health insurance for the urban-impoverished. However, the application process is a deterrent for citizens who are marginally literate. Without convenient transportation they only have access to near-by medical facilities. Those facilities are normally under-staffed and over-used.

I have taken urban-impoverished patients to the only health care facility within driving distance that will treat them. Waiting areas are full of patients, some seriously ill, waiting to be seen by medical staff. The over-worked staff is often neither friendly nor helpful. Learning a particular institution's protocol can be exasperating. Facilities are huge and complex. I've watched the poor wait for hours only to discover they were waiting in the wrong area. Such medical facilities do what they can to comfort and heal patients. Sometimes it is not enough. Sophisticated procedures like heart surgery are not available to the uninsured and underinsured.

Entertainment

For those focused on survival, release from reality is not only desirable, it is necessary. Typical inner city entertainment includes extended hours of watching television, playing video games or hangin' and rappin' with the bro' for a "minute." ("Minute" is inner city slang that can refer to any time period.) Entertainment is frequent, normally daily. Boredom sometimes leads to much less wholesome entertainment like sexual abuse or other mischievous and criminal behavior.

The inner-urban home has constant background noise with a television, radio, or CD player blasting. Conversation is very participatory with more than one person talking at a time. It is not deemed rude or really even interruptive to talk while you are listening to someone else.

Personality is a major source of entertainment. Anyone with the ability to hold the attention of others by telling stories or jokes will be well liked. Conversation is nearly always about people, never about work or school.

Some foods are consumed as entertainment catalysts. High concentrations of sugar, caffeine, and alcohol help many escape the day's ills. Consumption of these exacerbates the nutritional deficiency.

Dependency

Most inner-city people are dependent. What they depend on varies but they are dependent on something or someone. Drugs, alcohol, and sex are frequent dependencies. The urban-impoverished can also become dependent on the very government, social services, or individuals that are trying to help them become independent. Rather than help eliminate client's problems, often support people and systems unintentionally perpetuate their problems by assuming responsibility.

Survival

Survival is a full time activity for inner city residents. Their waking hours are spent searching for something to trade or get a little cash any way they can to pay rent, utility bills, and grocery bills. They frequent all the thrift shops and places that give handouts. Making regular rounds of government assistance agencies and charities is very time consuming. Every agency and charity has rules to learn and forms to complete. Waiting lines are usually long. Unexpected emergencies are normal. It can take days to solve a seemingly simple problem.

Inner city poor learn to manipulate the system to stay alive. Some are very adept at playing on the emotions of agency personnel with their portfolio of excuses and diversional tactics. Though often pigeonholed as less intelligent, they are smart and quickly learn the chinks in the bureaucratic armor.

Quizzes

Take the following quizzes published by aha! Process, Inc. to help understand the inner city. (24/ Payne) Take the first one to understand what you would need to know to survive poverty. Then, take the second one to understand what those in poverty do not know. Put a check by each item you know how to do.

Could you survive poverty?

1. I know which churches and sections of town have the best rummage sales.
2. I know which rummage sales have "bag sales" and when.
3. I know which grocery stores' garbage bins can be accessed for thrown-away food.
4. I know how to get someone out of jail.
5. I know how to physically fight and defend myself physically.
6. I know how to get a gun, even if I have a police record.
7. I know how to keep my clothes from being stolen at the Laundromat.
8. I know what problems to look for in a used car.
9. I know how to live without a checking account.
10. I know how to live without electricity and a phone.
11. I know how to use a knife as scissors.
12. I can entertain a group of friends with my personality and my stories.
13. I know what to do when I don't have money to pay the bills.
14. I know how to move in half a day.
15. I know how to get and use food stamps or an electronic card for benefits.
16. I know where the free medical clinics are.
17. I am very good at trading and bartering.
18. I can get by without a car.

Can you survive in middle class?

1. I know how to get my children into Little League, piano lessons, soccer, etc.
2. I know how to set a table properly.
3. I know which stores are most likely to carry the clothing brands my family wears.
4. My children know the best name brands in clothing.
5. I know how to order in a nice restaurant.
6. I know how to use a credit card, checking account, and savings account – and I understand an annuity. I understand term life insurance, disability insurance, and 20/80 medical insurance policy, as well as house insurance, flood insurance, and replacement insurance.
7. I talk to my children about going to college.
8. I know how to get one of the best interest rates on my new-car loan.
9. I understand the difference among principal, interest, and escrow statements on my house payment.
10. I know how to help my children with their homework and do not hesitate to call the school if I need additional information.
11. I know how to decorate the house for the different holidays.
12. I know how to get a library card.
13. I know how to use most of the tools in the garage.
14. I repair items in my house almost immediately when they break – or know a repair service and call it.

Used by permission from aha! Process, Inc. 800-424-9484
www.ahaprocess.com

Faces

It's important for you to know that the people in the inner city are precious. I hope that being factual did not

27

make me appear to be overly critical. Many lovely people are inner-urban dwellers. They may be unlike you, but wonderful people just the same. I'm sure you have seen photos or videos showing people in poverty. They are not just pictures; these are people with real needs, real desires and real challenges. Trading locations with an inner-urban dweller would not change who we are but our new circumstances (the "face" of our surroundings) would greatly change our expression.

Facial expressions can be deceiving. Almost everyone has learned to at times hide what is going on within them. Let's next look behind the inner city's face, look inside. Check out the values that drive behaviors. Poor urbanites do not value what the rest of America values. I don't mean baseball, hot dogs, and apple pie. I rather mean such things as achievement, wealth, and education.

Inner City Summary

- 76.1 million families (46.2 million people) in poverty
- Residents are half as likely to own their home
- Most children do not live with both parents
- Fatherless children are prone to trouble
- Have much higher crime rates than in other areas
- High school graduation rate is country's lowest
- Necessities cost more
- Transportation is less convenient
- Employees are not secure
- Income is not sufficient for necessities
- Residents are less healthy
- Daily entertainment is imperative
- Dependency is rampant
- Survival takes full-time effort

PART TWO: WHO OR WHAT MADE IT THIS WAY?

The culture of the inner city is very different from the rest of America. Other cultures take time, patience, and objectivity to understand. I worked in the American subsidiary of a foreign company and traveled to several foreign countries. I learned to identify the key differences of other cultures and adapt to them. Americans that haven't traveled beyond our borders usually either expect that people everywhere live like we do or at least wish they could. Untraveled Americans assume that everyone acknowledges that the American way is the best way. When Americans of such mind-set encounter another culture they get frustrated and can be very critical.

Cultures are determined by the values of their people. American values are neither global nor necessarily better than other values.

During my first trip to Europe I was very frustrated at the transportation hubs such as train stations and airports. I was shoved waiting for my luggage at the baggage claim, preempted at the snack bar, and bumped into waiting at the ticket counter. I first thought the nationals had intentionally selected me on which to demonstrate their disrespect for Americans. Then I noticed that they were also bumping and shoving each other. At the conclusion of that trip I returned home telling everyone who would listen how rude Europeans are.

A wise colleague suggested that before my next trip I read a good book about the culture in the country I was to visit. I did and learned many cultural differences including that standing in line and waiting for others are not global norms. In many countries that have been crowded for years it is not considered rude to force your way through crowds. It is rather considered normal, necessary and acceptable.

Personal space is smaller in densely populated countries.

It became obvious that we don't all have similar values. Once I accepted that my values aren't universal or even always better, I could survive in and actually enjoy other cultures.

We already know that the impoverished don't live like we do. Chapter two lists the internal forces that make them live differently. As you read please avoid the tendency to condemn them or their values.

THE FORCE - The Inner City Value System
(Chapter two)

The culture in the inner city is very different from the rest of America. Being different doesn't necessarily equate to being bad or wrong, rather just different.

I can't, and doubt that anyone can, fully explain why the inner city is the way it is. Causality is broad and the forces are strong. I will, however, explain what I can.

At the root of all science is causality, the law of cause and effect: every cause has a definite effect and every effect has a definite cause. All scientific laws build on this foundational truth; no causality, no science. Newton's first law of motion states that in order for the motion of an object to change, a force must act upon it, a concept generally called inertia. Ok, I know, social science isn't governed by the laws of physics. But, wait, isn't it true that unless some force acts on us we continue moving in the same direction?

A force is a compulsion or constraint exerted upon or against a person or thing. Our values are strong social forces. Values are principles, standards, or qualities considered worthwhile or desirable. A person's values are visceral; deep inward feelings. They affect who people are and what they do. Values are the internal forces that forge the inner city. Values motivate our decisions. Life's decisions have profound impact. We make our decisions, and then our decisions make us. Let that sink in. When we make decisions, choose one option, then the consequences of that option further shape us.

The values of the urban-impoverished are different

31

from those in other circumstances, in other cultures. Ruby K. Payne, Ph.D., Philip DeVol, and Terie Dreussi Smith compare the values of the Poverty Class, the Middle Class, and the Wealthy in their book *Bridges Out of Poverty*. (25/ Payne) Read it. My experience validates their assertions.

Describe your neighborhood. Why is it like that? Why do you do what you do?

It's difficult to understand the values of others without identifying our own values. Since most people who personally interact with the Impoverished are Middle Class, let us compare and contrast the Impoverished Class's values to the Middle Class's values. In this book the word impoverished means people in generational poverty. Payne, DeVol and Smith define generational poverty as those who have "been in poverty for at least two generations." (25/ Payne, page 65) They are distinctly different from those in situational poverty who "lack resources due to a particular event (i.e., a death, chronic illness, divorce, et cetera.)" People in situational poverty may or may not have the same values as those in generational poverty. The majority of people in the hood come from many generations of poverty.

It is important to distinguish long-term inner city residents from those who are passing through. New arrivals from other countries such as Latin America, Africa, or Asia often come to America and are temporarily inner city residents. They are just passing through the inner city as they get oriented and adapt to a new country. They will neither live there nor be impoverished for multiple generations and do not display the characteristics common to long-termers.

The values discussed here are prevalent in each class but may not apply to one hundred percent of those in the class. These values are American values. Societies in other countries may have different values.

These values should enlighten you. After I spent months trying to determine what made the hood the way it is, I discovered these values. They helped assemble the puzzle for me – they are the force that changed the direction of my understanding and my effort.

Here we go. I'll first define each value then discuss its significance.

Driving Force

The driving force in life is that value that occupies most of our time, attention, and energy. It is the over-arching value; the major social motivator. Other values are driven by it. Payne, DeVol, and Smith wrote that the driving force for the Middle Class is "work and achievement." (25/ Payne, page 58) This can be seen in nearly every aspect of Middle Class life: in business, in school, in athletics, in social clubs, in the family and even in church.

Middle Classers are constantly trying to accomplish something. Their sense of worth is dependent upon self-evaluation of their achievements. When you meet someone new, what do you ask them? After first asking their name the second and third questions are "what do you do" and "where do you live?" Why do we ask these? To measure ourselves versus them we compare levels of achievement. Their occupation and neighborhood are the major indicators of relative achievement. Having rated ourselves in comparison to them, we know how to relate to them.

Middle Classers view their vocations as paths for achievement. Few are satisfied in the current position. Surrounded by the trappings provided by past successes, they plot a path to greater achievement as if it were their reason to live. They climb from position to position to exhibit achievement. It may appear to be the pursuit of money but money is not the objective. Money is a medium to be exchanged for items that symbolize achievement. Trappings are really trophies of a particular level of success.

Try to identify an area of your life in which achievement is not the driving force. It is so much a part of you that you probably assume that it is innate and universal, common to all people in all classes.

Not so among the impoverished. Payne, DeVol and Smith wrote that the impoverished are focused on "survival." (25/ Payne, page 58) To the poor, survival is staying alive until tomorrow: eating enough to survive, being warm enough or cool enough to survive, getting life-sustaining medications and avoiding life-threatening violence. Survival to the impoverished is not superficial; it is mortal.

When meeting someone the impoverished don't ask "what do you do" or "where do you live"? They more likely ask "who is your family?" Relationships are more valuable to them than achievement.

I was surprised to learn how consuming survival is. It occupies all their time, attention, and energy! Imagine how time consuming and energy sapping it is to quell hunger pangs, maintain at least moderate health and avoid bodily harm for yourself and your loved-ones in high-density, low income, violence-prone living areas.

Rather than a theater in which to perform achievements, impoverished workers view work as only a tool to obtain what is necessary for survival. Money is a tool but valued differently from the Middle Class. Their view of money is discussed later. The effort they expend at work is based on how well they like the boss, not how well they like the work. Any loyalty they may feel is to the boss, not the work or the company. If they do not like the boss they will eventually quit. Current feelings are more important to them than future circumstances.

World View

World-view is the overall perspective from which one sees and interprets the world around them, a collection of beliefs about life and the universe, which is held by an individual or a group. It is our perception of the "world" that controls us and determines what we think we control.

Payne, DeVol and Smith wrote that the Middle Class "sees the world in terms of national setting." (25/ Payne, page 58) The Middle Class believes that the nation directly impacts them and they directly impact the nation. Thus, the nation, the other people of the nation, and the events throughout the nation change their life in some way. They also believe that their individual achievements, jobs, businesses, faith, and social involvement in some way change the nation in which they live.

Not so among the impoverished. Payne, DeVol and Smith wrote that the impoverished "see the world in terms of a local view," a neighborhood-based or hood-based view. (25/ Payne, page 58) The impoverished believe that only their hood, the other people of their hood and the events in their hood affect them. The only place they expect to affect is their hood.

Worldview appears to coincide with area of travel. Most in the Middle Class have traveled much of the nation and many have traveled to other countries. It's not clear which came first, the national worldview or the travel, but the correlation is obvious.

Many inner-urban residents have never been outside their neighborhood. Take, for instance, Ronald, an early teen that I have taken to sporting events. Ronald is an inner city anomaly in that he lives with both his father and stepmother. His father is dying of cancer. He, his stepmother, and his younger brother struggle through each day. I took Ronald to an AAA baseball game. He had previously only been to one baseball game and that was his seven-year-old cousin's T-ball game. During the AAA game his head was on a swivel trying to take it all in. He never stopped asking questions. Everything fascinated him - the game, the players, the uniforms, the scoreboard, the food, and so forth. That may have been the most fun I have ever had at a baseball game! Like many inner city kids, Ronald seldom gets out of his neighborhood.

Former U.S. Attorney General Robert F. Kennedy said, "There are those who look at things the way they are, and ask why... I dream of things that never were, and ask why not." We all tend to react to how we think things are. World view determines or describes the basis for how we think things are. In a culture that has less exposure to other places and cultures the world view is a closely cropped photo. Less exposure to other lifestyles makes dreaming of things that never were more difficult.

Destiny

Destiny is the inevitable or necessary fate to which a particular person or thing is consigned, the power or agency thought to predetermine events. It is what makes you do what you do and what controls who you are. Payne, DeVol and Smith wrote that Middle Class members "believe in choice." (25/ Payne, page 58) The Middle Class believes they "can change (the) future with good choices." They are free to choose who they are and what they do. This class believes that life is an endless chain of choices. A great phrase many use is – you aren't born a winner, you aren't born a looser, you are born a chooser. When life goes sour, Middle Classers point to the bad decisions that caused the bad results.

Since their choices affect the future, Middle Class members post-evaluate choices and modify the way they make future choices. Decision making ability is constantly honed.

Not so for the impoverished. Payne, DeVol and Smith wrote that they "believe in fate." (25/ Payne, page 58) They "cannot do much to mitigate chance." They are controlled by chance. They do not believe that they can change much about their life. They think that life keeps smacking them back to where they came from. They are not normally aware of choices or decisions. Believing to be controlled by fate, they do not evaluate previous choices to improve future decisions.

It was a shock that since they were born poor, they believe they must live poor and will die poor!

Middle Class people recognize alternatives and options but the impoverished do not. They are not aware of the need to make choices; they just react to the current situation. The ramifications of actions are unnoticed.

The urban impoverished are frequently frustrated by negative consequences in their lives, yet, they don't connect them to choices they made. Example, all the ex-cons that I met claimed that they will never return to jail. However, the recidivism rate is above eighty percent. They return to the same friends in the same hood and take the same actions that previously resulted in their incarceration. When re-arrested they don't examine their actions but rather blame what they believe are absurd laws or biased law enforcement or they just consider it their fate in life. Why? Because they believe that life is controlled by chance and nothing they do will change the outcome.

There's an old story that you can train fleas to live in an open-top jar by first keeping them in a jar with a transparent lid. After they have jumped and hit the clear lid several times, they stop trying. Many impoverished people act as if they were trained in an open-topped jar. They don't try to change their circumstances because they don't think they can. They just try to survive them.

Social Emphasis

Social Emphasis is one's primary social purpose. It determines acceptance and relationship to others in society. Payne, DeVol and Smith wrote that for those in the Middle Class the social "emphasis is on self-governance and self-sufficiency." (25/ Payne, page 58) From childhood those in the Middle Class are taught to make it on their own, not to depend on anyone else. Many of their actions and possessions are chosen to demonstrate to others that they have it all together, are self-sufficient and don't need help from anyone.

Middle Class members are reluctant to ask for personal assistance. They think asking for social or financial help is a sign of weakness.

Not so for the impoverished. Payne, DeVol and Smith

wrote that their social emphasis is "inclusion of people he/she likes." (25/ Payne, page 58) The impoverished want to be included. They struggle to show that they are valuable and that they deserve a place in this world. They are frustrated by what appear to be attempts by other classes to exclude them. The only Middle Classers that they encounter may be front-line people at social services. Since the middle class rules appear designed to keep them from socially advancing, they assume the people administering those rules are trying to ostracize them. The impoverished react negatively more to the rules of an agency than to the values of social workers.

Asking other impoverished people for help is not a sign of weakness, but rather of resourcefulness and evidence of ability to survive. They help each other thereby including each other.

Their need to be included is so strong that if family does not include and value them, they will find someone who does. The most frequent substitute for biological family is a gang. Gangs are very adept at fostering loyalty and a strong sense of belonging.

Power and Respect

Power is the ability or capacity to perform or act effectively, the ability or official capacity to exercise control, authority. Respect is the feeling or demonstration of deferential regard for, esteem, to avoid violation of or interference with. Payne, DeVol and Smith did not compare these values.

It seems apparent that Middle Classers base power and respect on level of achievement in areas such as education, social status, wealth, employer, career path, neighborhood, home value, and make of automobiles. Restating a previous example, one of the first questions usually asked when meeting a person is, "what do you do?" The answer will be evaluated and a value assigned to the person so that we know who has the most power and is due the most respect in this relationship.

Conflict pushes power and respect to the surface. Middle Class members respond to conflict by negotiating. The relative positions and skills of the participants determine the power they exhibit and the respect they receive. Preserving and leveraging position is more important than feelings. The extreme of this phenomenon is played out daily in our Courts. Litigation is the ultimate battle of power and respect.

Not so for the impoverished. Power and respect are dependent on the individual's ability to entertain others or help them survive rather than accomplishments.

For the impoverished power and respect are personality based not achievement based. The relative power and respect afforded an inner city woman depends on her level of skill at providing and protecting others. Single moms with many kids are revered. The relative power and respect afforded an urban impoverished man often springs from ability to entertain or intimidate others. Good rappers and break-dancers are esteemed more for their ability to entertain others than for their skill. Gang-bangers exert influence by intimidation not by achievement.

Here conflict is not settled through negotiation. Seldom do the urban poor have conflict-resolution skills. If conflict is not resolved in favor of the most likeable (respected) person, it will be settled in favor of the most intimidating (powerful) person via threats. It may result in an assault.

Some inner-urban dwellers use atypical dress styles or expensive items to entertain or intimidate others. Their "bling" is very showy jewelry and automobile accessories. These are not trophies of achievement but rather are symbols of power and due respect.

Love and Acceptance

Love is a deep, tender, ineffable feeling of affection and solicitude toward a person, such as that arising from kinship, recognition of attractive qualities, or a sense of underlying oneness. Acceptance is favorable reception, approval. Love and acceptance always depend on something. Payne, DeVol and Smith wrote that in the Middle Class "love and acceptance (are) conditional and based largely upon achievement." (25/ Payne, page 58) Middle Class achievement normally results in approval. Even achieving Middle Class children are given an open display of love and affection. Every new skill demonstration is celebrated with a hug and "at-a boy" or "good girl." Achievement is encouraged, occasionally worshiped. High achievement almost automatically results in acceptance by most of the class.

Not so for the impoverished. Payne, DeVol and Smith wrote "love and acceptance (are) conditional, based upon whether (an) individual is liked." (25/ Payne, page 58) Similar to power and respect, love and acceptance are based on the individual rather than what he or she accomplishes. Ability to help others survive or release them temporarily from the struggle via entertainment results in love and acceptance.

Family Structure

Family structure is the predominant method of

41

governance, the order of authority within a family. Payne, DeVol and Smith wrote that for the Middle Class family structure "tends to be patriarchal." (25/ Payne, page 58) Fathers are the main protectors, main providers, and the final authority.

The value that others place on a Middle Class father is often imputed to his family. As middle class jobs have become less and less physical this value has moderated somewhat. Yet, fathers are still primary protectors and providers while mothers are primary nurturers. Frequently Middle Class members ask a child, "what does your father do?" Or ask a woman, "what does your husband do?"

Not so for the impoverished. Payne, DeVol and Smith wrote that impoverished family structure "tends to be matriarchal." (25/ Payne, page 58) The mother is routinely the protector, the provider, and the final authority.

The impoverished family is viewed in the light of the mother. It would be abnormal for an inner city resident to ask, "What does your mother do?" Achievement and position are not important. They rather ask, "How many live in your home?" or "what is your mother like?" These draw out who mom is, not what she does.

Whatever may come, impoverished mothers are expected to provide and protect. Many women are abused by their men but still cling to them. They do not escape abuse but rather consider it a normal part of their fate. As a contrary, abusing a woman's children is seldom tolerated.

Inner city men are expected to be very macho: good lovers and good fighters. Men use women rather than establishing lasting relationships with them. Male worth is typically proven by their love-making and fighting skills. Very few inner-urban families have a functioning father in the home. Many of the children have never seen their biological father and may not even know his name.

Possessions

Possessions are items actually held or occupied with or without rightful ownership, the things we own or, at least, of which we have beneficial use. Payne, DeVol and Smith wrote that Middle Class people possess "things" or items – usually the more, the better. (25/ Payne, page 58) The Middle Class philosophy described by the trite saying "he who dies with the most toys wins," is pervasive. Possessions are trophies of achievement.

For Middle Classers much of a thing's value is "in the having." Some joy comes from the process of acquisition but possession verifies achievement. Look in their homes to see many items that are unused or underused. Items are collected and displayed. Many in this class willingly sacrifice time with family and loved-ones to accumulate more items.

Not so for the impoverished. Most items are not valued by the impoverished because they are in constant jeopardy of being eaten by vermin, damaged by weather, consumed by fire, stolen, lost or broken. Inner city poor believe that people can be possessed and that people are not as vulnerable as things. Payne, DeVol and Smith wrote that "people" are their most coveted possession. (25/ Payne, page 58)

A young man must have his "woman." A young woman must have her "man." She displays her man like a prize. Babies are "owned", very valuable trophies. Teen girls pine for a baby that will be theirs to keep. The impoverished are very possessive of all the people they like. People have such importance that time with them is not normally sacrificed to acquire things. Relationships take precedence over accumulating items.

Due to vulnerability, their few valued possessions in the hood are clung to tightly. Anything treasured will be protected, even physically if necessary. Everyone else is assumed to similarly protect what they value.

Occasionally someone visiting the inner city will briefly leave one of their possessions unattended. When they return it is gone. They are aghast that it has been taken, stolen. Whoever took it probably did not think they were stealing. They likely believed that the person who left it unattended did not place much value on it. Anything left unguarded is assumed unwanted and available to the first taker! To those who have little and who have learned to guard what they have, this is not stealing. It's being resourceful. It's survival.

I watched this happen repeatedly. Volunteers from the 'burbs would come to help do maintenance or construction projects on in-hood facilities. At break or lunch they left their tools where they were working only to arrive later to fewer, if any, tools. Occasionally we were able to identify who had taken the tools and confront them. They admitted having them but admitted no guilt explaining that they assumed no one wanted them.

Money

Money is a medium that can be exchanged for goods and services, official currency, coins, and negotiable paper notes issued by a government. The value given it varies and so do it's' uses. Payne, DeVol and Smith wrote that the Middle Class views money as "to be managed." (25/ Payne, page 58) Money is to be used to acquire things, to be invested, and to be multiplied. Middle class members are constantly trading-up for better possessions, even by using debt financing.

Middle Class money is not just an exchange medium it is an asset used to measure achievement. Members of this class "work" money, they acquire it, multiply it, and exchange it for long-term security and comfort. Purchased items indicate the owner's level of achievement as best seen in size and location of home(s) and makes and models of automobiles. The appetite for expensive items outpaces the ability to fund them. It is impolite to ask someone about their income but it is normal to speculate on someone else's income based on what they possess.

Not so for the impoverished. Payne, DeVol and Smith wrote that money is "to be used, spent." (25/ Payne, page 58) Like any other possession, money is vulnerable. It may soon be lost, damaged, burned, or stolen. Since it may be gone tomorrow, it is imperative to use it today. Ways are found immediately to use all they have. Unexpected money is instantly gone – it is spent before it can disappear. Hence, to members of other social classes many of their purchases appear foolhardy.

To the impoverished the future is a mirage, money is exchanged for immediate gratification. Items that are normally cost-prohibitive such as expensive clothes, jewelry, beverages, or entertainment have more value than accumulated cash.

By the way, it is significant that the impoverished are very generous to their peers. Cash-on-hand may be shared with family or friends in the hood rather than hoarded.

Time

Time is a nonspatial continuum in which events occur in apparently irreversible succession from the past through the present to the future, an interval separating two points on this continuum, duration. The value of time varies by class. Payne, DeVol and Smith wrote that for those in the Middle Class the "future (is) most important." "Decisions (are) made against future ramifications." (25/ Payne, page 58)The Middle Class works hard and plays hard to build a better future for themselves and their offspring. The future is valuable enough to warrant present sacrifice.

For the Middle Class time, like money, is an asset to be managed – to be acquired, invested, and multiplied. Timesaving devices are valued. Since the future is most valuable, spending additional time today to benefit tomorrow is wise.

Not so for the impoverished. Payne, DeVol and Smith wrote that "present (is) most important. Decisions (are) made for (the) moment based on feelings or survival." (25/ Payne, page 58) The only certain moment is the current one. Tomorrow may never come! Long-range Impoverished Class plans are much nearer-by than those of the Middle Class. Their future plan may be what to do tomorrow or this weekend rather than how to have a more stable life-style in the future years.

Time is relative to the impoverished and only has emotional importance. They don't recognize that time can be acquired, invested, or multiplied. Time saving and efficiency are not important. Time comes and goes as fate dictates.

Relationships are much more important to the impoverished than tasks. Time is neither scheduled nor treasured. Starting times and ending times are determined by the Middle Class and consequently treated by the impoverished as arbitrary and relative. This value is manifest in disregard for scheduled meeting times and work hours.

Middle-class people often become very frustrated working in the hood with residents who are frequently late to or are absent from meetings. Interruptions are the norm as their present-time focus drives their demands.

Education

Education is the act or process of educating or being educated, the knowledge or skill obtained or developed by a learning process, a program of instruction of a specified kind or level. Education is the process of learning those facts, processes, and procedures that help us understand life and how to live it. Payne, DeVol and Smith wrote that the Middle Class regards education as "crucial for climbing (the) success ladder and making money." (25/ Payne, page 58) The Middle Class believes that the better educated they are the more they achieve: the higher they climb on the corporate ladder, the more money they make and the more trophies they accumulate.

Whether education has an immediate benefit is not very important to Middle Classers. Education, like money and time, is an asset to be acquired, invested, and multiplied. They value what education can produce more than knowledge itself. The educational process develops structures and habits that translate to skills with future value.

Not so for the impoverished. They see no reward for education. Payne, DeVol and Smith wrote that it is "valued and revered as abstract but not as reality." (25/ Payne, page 58) It does not appear to have any immediate value; it doesn't help them survive today.

In the inner city results must be immediate. Even chronic needs are not regarded until they are acute. The impoverished do not recognize any immediate survival-value in education. Like money and time, education's value is only viewed in the light of today.

This is a new concept for me. Think back to your elementary education. Now remember your secondary education. What did you learn on each given day that helped you survive that day? To the impoverished the future will only be important after they make it through today. Why prepare to seize tomorrow's opportunities when you don't believe there will be any and you doubt that you will survive to see tomorrow anyway?

The graduation rates were presented in the Education section of Chapter One. This helps to understand why they are so low.

Entertainment

Entertainment is the act of amusing or occupying someone; a temporary release from the rigors of life. Payne, DeVol and Smith do not compare these values. It's apparent that the Middle Class values entertainment as scheduled recreation activity that often has an achievement element.

The type and place of entertainment are metrics of achievement. For example, to the Middle Class, vacationing at a Hawaiian beach hotel signals to others a higher level of achievement than vacationing at a low cost in-state motel. If the entertainment involves competition such as golfing or skiing or fishing, achievement is always involved. Even when spectating, the achievement level of the team or artist watched is important. Celebrities in sport, art, politics, etc. draw crowds who strut their attendance before peers.

Like money, time, and education, entertainment is to be acquired, managed, and multiplied. Recreation is planned ahead, prepared for, sacrificed for, and savored.

Not so for the impoverished. Entertainment is a part of surviving, a necessary daily relief from stress. Entertainment fills any available time and often consists of endless hours of watching television or playing video games or talking with friends.

Since the poor's struggle for survival is very stressful, the need for release from stress is frequent and acute. Imagine that you spend every hour awake worrying about surviving and manipulating others to assure that you do. Do you think daily entertainment would be necessary for coping with these consuming stresses? It is for them.

Major Stressors

Major stressors are the primary agents, conditions, or other stimuli that cause mental anguish. These are the influences on our lives that create the most internal pressure. A cause of major stress for Middle Class members is time management or maybe more specifically, dealing with time uses that cannot be controlled, that seem to control them. For the Middle Class achievement is time-bound. Unplanned time usage at best delays achievement and at worst threatens it.

Not so for the impoverished. The Middle Class rules that control business and government cause major stress for the impoverished. These Middle Class rules are based on Middle Class values that are considered arbitrary, relative and unnatural for the impoverished. In some cases these rules really do make their survival more difficult.

The psychosomatic results of stress are well documented. Stress has many negative biological effects but has at least one positive social impact. It eventually motivates change!

General

I am glad that we have more than one class in America. I really enjoy my relationships in both the Impoverished and Middle Classes. I acknowledge the values of others and their right to set them. Rather than eliminating the Impoverished Class I advocate empowering it.

Matrix

At the end of this chapter is a matrix of Class Values for the Impoverished and Middle Class. It summarizes the previously compared values. It is similar but not identical to, a matrix in *Bridges Out of Poverty* by Ruby K. Payne, Ph.D., Philip DeVol, and Terie Dreussi Smith.

Having reviewed the external expression of the inner city and forces that make it the way it is, a natural question is "what is being done about it?" We will explore that next.

Class Values
Values drive Hidden Rules within Classes

Impoverished	Middle Class
Driving Force: Survival	Achievement
World View: Neighborhood based	Nationally based
Destiny: Controlled by fate	Determined by choice
Social Emphasis: Inclusion	Self-sufficiency
Power or Respect: Based on individual	Based on position
Love & Acceptance Based on individual likeability	Achievement based
Family Structure: Matriarchal	Patriarchal
Possessions: People	Things
Money: To be spent	To be managed
Time: Present most important	Future most important
Education: Abstract, no immediate value	Crucial for climbing
Entertainment: Daily to relive stress	Planned in advance
Major Stressors: Middle-class rules* that complicate survival	Time Management

* Business & Government run on Middle Class rules

PART THREE: WE KEEP IT THIS WAY!

The Missions committee at Commontown Community Church is discussing where they will send their work team for the annual summer project.

Sympathetic Sarah says, "I think we should go to downtown Chicago and help the ghetto people." "Oh", replies Assistant Pastor Pragmatic Paul, "We did that two years ago. It wasn't a very good trip." Energetic Edmund asks, "why not?" "Well", explains Paul, "first of all they didn't have a decent place for us to stay! The first night we slept on the pews in the sanctuary at Miraculous Municipal Mission. It was awful! It was filthy and the air conditioner didn't work right, it was so hot! There were only two small bathrooms, not nearly enough for our group. The kitchen only had one little sink and a small microwave. Fortunately we found a decent motel about ten miles away so we stayed there and just went to the mission in the afternoons. They really didn't have much worthwhile for us to do. They wanted us to clean the place, even the bathrooms, and paint. We wanted to tell those poor people about Jesus!

This year let's go where we can lead a lot of people to Christ in our five days!" "Ya', I was on that ministry team", injected Judgmental Jenny. "The residents really didn't seem to care that they live in squalor and sin! I don't think they can be helped anyway. Why don't they just get a job and stop shootin' up?"

Sound familiar? Have you ever experienced such a summer project or been to a similar meeting? Have you wondered while watching the news, "what's wrong with them; why don't they just straighten up or at least get out of there?" Look next at the external forces that prevent residents' change.

THE FIXERS – Those Influencing The Inner City (Chapter three)

A fixer is someone who intervenes to enable another person to circumvent an intrinsic outcome. Inner city fixers are organizations and individuals trying to help the residents. A few are scoundrels who see an opportunity to prey on desperate poor-urbanites, but most really want to help. They see "the problem" and are determined to solve it.

There are countless programs and services intended to improve life for those in the inner city. To list them all would take many pages. I could not locate reliable numbers of various social service providers nationally. Recent research revealed an example that helps "scope" their availability: Saint Louis, Missouri. Washington University's web site lists about 750 different social service agencies in the St. Louis area. (26/ Community Service) Washington University's Community Service Office's web site lists about 406 different Nonprofit Organizations in Saint Louis. (27/ Washington University) St. Louis is representative of large metropolitan areas; it struggles with inner-urban problems and has a plethora of fixers. It is apparent that the number of organizations trying to change any given inner city is in the hundreds.

Fixers divide neatly into three categories: government agencies, private nonprofit organizations, and individuals.

Government Agencies

Many social programs and services are government run. Using simple arithmetic we can estimate that Saint Louis has about 344 government agencies, 750 minus 406. Since 344 is slightly less than half of 750, it appears that nearly half of the listed social services in St. Louis are government run. That gives an order-of-magnitude ratio. We can assume that the ratio is similar in other cities.

Government programs are typically larger than other programs such that government may account for more than half the impact on the inner city. Though government organizations only provide about half of all the services, they also control many others through funding. Many non-government programs and organizations receive public money to help fund the services they provide. Government funding brings government oversight and some inherent constraints. Social services directly affect inner-urban dwellers. Thus, government has a huge impact on social services and on the urban-impoverished.

The common service areas offered by government include unemployment insurance, job training, family advocacy, temporary assistance to needy families, public health education, counseling for mental disorders, Medicaid, and STD education and testing. These services are paramount to the poor, the elderly, and the infirm. A high percentage of such people live in the inner city.

Government is normally better funded and staffed than other organizations to deliver some of these programs and services. However, some programs would be better offered by families, neighborhoods, churches, and communities rather than being abdicated to government. Some government employees work vigorously and consider their work to be their mission in life. To others it is just employment or a career.

Some clients receive government assistance gladly and respectfully. Others are skeptical and guarded, making it difficult to help them.

Government programs and services all follow a pattern. In general, election-driven politicians and mostly well-meaning bureaucrats develop these programs. Most are doing the best they can with the approach they take. Others appear to be more concerned about their own careers than about social change. Politicians and bureaucrats are normally middle class individuals using results from middle class-developed research to design programs that are implemented by middle-classers according to middle class rules. As previously discussed, these rules are confusing and unnatural to poor urbanites making them a deterrent to helping those most in need. This will be further explained chapter five.

These fixers neither live, nor have they ever lived, in the area they serve. Seldom are the impoverished intimately involved in program development. They may not be viewed as intelligent enough or well enough educated to be involved. Sometimes it is just too difficult and time consuming for middle-class social servants to adapt to the values of the impoverished, find the assets that exist in inner city neighborhoods, and leverage them for broader good. It takes a lot of relationship building to engage the impoverished and involve them. The impoverished must be convinced that they really can affect the future enough to warrant the time and effort; that they will be rewarded with immediate results.

Private Nonprofit Organizations

Nonprofit organizations (NPOs) are specially treated corporations that are formed to meet social needs, not for the purpose of making a profit. Nonprofit designation is received from the Federal Government. Contrary to common belief, these organizations are allowed to make a profit, but the profits are restricted. Each state has slightly different laws governing the enterprises from which NPOs can derive profit, what percent of their total revenue can come from profit making enterprises, and how those profits can be used.

Private nonprofit organizations routinely offer social services. It appears that over half of the social service organizations in most metropolitan areas are private NPOs. The number of these agencies is difficult to determine but it is estimated that there are hundreds in most cities.

Services typically provided by NPOs include budgeting help, employment assistance, health-care, substance abuse intervention, transitional housing, subsidized housing, legal assistance, adult education, life-skills training, and children's programs such as tutoring or arts or sports.

Often the services offered by private nonprofit organizations overlap and even compete with each other. They are reluctant to partner. Fund raising is competitive and fosters separation due to the belief that espousing another NPO may help validate them such that they attract more funders. With limited funders and limited funds, nonprofit organizations often chase funds by adding programs that appeal to willing funders.

Savvy funders have begun requiring their grantees to collaborate with other providers. This external motivation will encourage cooperation among service providers. Current collaborators have discovered the synergy of working together.

Private nonprofits are dissimilar from government programs in that the providers are neither election-driven nor bureaucratic. Their approach, however, is similar.

Generally their services are conceived, developed, and implemented by middle-class employees according to middle class rules. Seldom do those working in NPOs live in the neighborhood they serve.

Faith-based Organizations

Faith-based Organizations are a subset of private nonprofit organizations. They deserve separate explanation because of their uniqueness. Faith-based services are offered by organizations that were founded on religious faith. In America most of these organizations are based on Christian faith. No data have been found listing the ratio of Faith-based to other nonprofit organizations.

Christian organizations are divided into two groups: churches and Para-church organizations. Most people do not think of churches as nonprofit organizations but the legally organized ones are. Para-church organizations are Christian groups that are formed to help churches. The word "Para" is Greek meaning "to come along side of," and the word "church" is English meaning "a body or organization of religious believers."

Churches best offer faith-based services. Too often, however, the church has treated the inner city like the first century Jews treated Samaria. No good Jew would have respected a Samaritan. Similarly, today most good church people do not want to talk about, hear about, drive through, or work in the hood! Para-church organizations frequently allow churches to fund and control social agencies from outside the hood. Faith-based services are usually conceived, developed, and implemented by middle-classers in suburban churches and offered at their inner city satellites or by the Para-church ministries that they sponsor. They function according to middle class rules.

Services normally provided by faith-based groups include food pantries, soup kitchens, clothing pantries, furniture and furnishings pantries, housing for homeless, transitional housing for ex-convicts, housing for battered women and children, daycare for infants and toddlers, preschools, tutoring for children and teens, spiritual guidance and health-care.

Though motivated by faith, too often their approach is indistinguishable from government programs or other nonprofit organizations. A few faith-based workers live, work, and worship in the neighborhood they serve. They call themselves incarnate ministers and are actually missionaries. It is more common, however, for faith-based workers to commute from the comfort of the suburbs.

Faith-based organizations are making an impact equal to or more positive than their counterparts. One of the missing motivators in the lives of urban-impoverished people is faith. They have no faith, so they have no hope, so they don't think they can affect their own situation. Faith-based organizations by their very existence nurture faith in those who need it so desperately. These organizations are faith-based in that everything they do is, or should be, motivated by their faith. Faith begets faith. Faith lived out by these fixers is a "seed" for some and a model for others. Faith is a powerful force and will be further explained in chapter eight.

Faith-based organizations were considered suspect by government services and other nonprofit organizations until recent administrations trumpeted their value. Particularly George W. Bush, his campaign team, and his administration sought to validate faith-based organizations.

Individuals

A few individuals spend time in the inner city trying to help. They customarily work with a small group of people. They are limited in their breadth, but due to their depth, are the most effective of all. Some of these individuals choose to live in the hood. They counter the social trend by dwelling there rather than living in the suburbs and serving in the hood. Since they live in the same conditions, they are able to really understand the values and to react to the needs. They are American heroes.

Results

The inner city is very complex; hence, the problems are also very complex. Symptoms are obvious everywhere. A common tendency is to prematurely conclude that a given symptom is the problem. Of course, that is over simplifying. Just as in mathematics, the problem must be correctly stated before it can be correctly solved. Affecting even one symptom is difficult. Next look who's really being helped.

THE FANTASY- Who is really being helped?
(Chapter four)

Most current programs and services really are not helping the urban impoverished very much. If they were, we should see the conditions improving in the inner city and the number in generational poverty decreasing. Neither is happening. Who is really being helped? Maybe the fixers are.

Government and private nonprofit programs often unintentionally keep the people they serve dependent. Inner city residents become dependent on the very programs that were designed to "help" them and the people who run these programs.

Government programs and services are conceived, planned, implemented and supervised by politicians and bureaucrats. Most of them are middle classers; most of their constituents are middle classers. These programs are evaluated either by the bureaucrats themselves or by the middle class consultants that they hire. There is typically a substantial disconnect between the officially reported results and the perception of those being served. Let me illustrate.

I attended a town hall meeting about violence in a major inner city. The Mayor, a representative from the Governor's office, a State Senator, the Police Chief, three City Council Members, a couple of Neighborhood Association representatives, several social workers, several Pastors, and a multitude of neighbors and interested citizens participated. This group should know what is happening and how to respond.

Two contrasting pictures of the situation were presented. The first half of the meeting was a roundtable of the dignitaries. All speakers had been instructed to be brief and to focus on solutions. Each successive speaker explained what they believed was the problem, the solutions they were already implementing and reported their gains. I thought, "Wow, we are making progress and given more time and money we will succeed." During the second half of the meeting neighboring pastors and residents described what they believed to be an ever-worsening situation, the problems they saw, and then proposed other solutions. I thought these people must live in a different city from the first group of speakers. They so obviously had an opposite opinion of the status. They were desperate in their belief that the problem is still out of control and getting worse. Then I thought, "Wow, we are in deep trouble."

The impoverished are not being helped or aren't being helped in the right ways. Politicians justify their election and/or re-election with reports of pertinent new legislation that they supported. Bureaucrats expect to keep their positions and hopefully realize annual pay increases based on published results. News media sell copy by reporting both of these.

According to the National Center for Policy Analysis, "virtually all of our federal welfare programs are entitlement programs - AFDC, food stamps, Medicaid, etc. This means that people qualify for relief based on financial considerations alone." (28/ Idea House, page 1) "There is still much to be learned about the ways in which people respond to federal entitlement programs. However, it is clear that in helping people, federal welfare programs create negative incentives.

The welfare system discourages work and encourages dependency, single motherhood and the breakup of families. The underclass – replete with crime and other antisocial behavior – is subsidized and sustained by the welfare state." (28/ Idea House, page 5) Welfare payments increase with need: unemployment, single parenthood and large families.

Most private nonprofit programs and services are similar. Typical nonprofit programs and services are conceived, planned, implemented and supervised by degreed individuals, middle classers. These organizations expand their funding and volunteer bases by trumpeting the ever-increasing need and their constant increase in the number of clients served.

An organization really making progress solving root problems should eventually report that the number being served is decreasing. If there was a positive impact, wouldn't the number needing service eventually shrink?

I have watched the Boards of Directors of nonprofit organizations whose mission is to serve the inner city. These Boards are middle class and wealthy men and women, predominantly Caucasian, who express a passion to help the poor. When the messy business of finding root problems and their solutions drags on, they conclude that this is not what they envisioned and not where they want to spend their time and effort. Many quit in frustration just when they are well enough informed to make a difference.

Most faith-based organizations are racing around the same track. They function similarly except that they are "faith motivated." I have come to believe that many people of faith do more to help themselves than the subjects of their "missions."

While working at an inner city faith-based ministry I entertained many volunteers and volunteer groups. Too frequently it was very obvious that they had come to get warm fuzzies from doing good deeds for others. A frequent tip-off was that they arrived with video camera in hand and wanted to record more than to work. The impoverished were not really being helped. The people in these organizations and their donors were - they felt better about themselves.

Are all the programs and services negative? No. Should all the fixers stop? No. Their motivation needs to be applauded but their approach and methods need to be changed. Are we winning the battle for the hood? No, I do not think so. I don't even think that we are closer to identifying the real problems.

What is preventing victory or, at least, advancement? We will consider that in the next chapter.

THE FETTERS- The Inner City Constraints
(Chapter five)

A fetter is something that restricts or restrains. Fetters are external conditions, circumstances or forces that impede movement or change. Some inner-urban fetters have been identified; others may yet be discovered. It is not uncommon for middle-classers to ask, "why don't they change" or "why don't they just get out of there?" Neither changing nor relocating is as easy for inner-urban residents as you might imagine. See what external forces constrain them and make changing or leaving unlikely.

Agency Program and Service Goals

Most programs and services exhibit two common flaws. First, they are focused on helping more individuals every year. Reports from both government and private nonprofit organizations justify their existence and make their plea for funds based on the continual growth in number of people served. Funders measure agency effectiveness with business metrics. Grantors respond favorably to increasing ratios of clients served per staff member and per budget dollar spent. The flaw is that an organization really making progress should at some juncture be reporting that the number being served is decreasing. Real success is eliminating some of the need so that the number needing service decreases.

Most agencies acquiesce to funders wishes. In order to grow their funding they focus on serving more clients. This typically consumes most of the creativity and energy that should have been spent identifying and eliminating causes of source problems. Helping a few be free from poverty is superior to helping many stay in it.

Suppose an agency exists to provide financial help with utility bill payment for those who are in danger of utility shut-off. This is a very forthright purpose. The agency has grown annually and boasts that the number they serve has increased at a steady twenty percent per year for the past five years. Impressive. Unfortunately there is something wrong with this picture. Constant increase in the need and number assisted does not indicate that the problem is being solved. It would be better to decrease the need by eliminating at least one cause of utility shut-offs. Permanently helping a few would be more effective than temporarily helping many.

I recall proudly displaying the continual growth pattern of an inner city ministry at which I served. When a funder responded by rating our growth versus the growth of all the other potential grantees, I had an epiphany. If we are really making a difference why are we all continually growing?

Second, these programs and services are developed and run by middle class social servants. Their goal is to get inner-urban dwellers up and out of the hood. That's the wrong goal! These are the very people that are most able to help others. They are more capable than an outsider to permanently help their peers. Continually taking the successful out of the hood removes the best role models, steals the leaders, and prevents leveraging their achievements to help others. These are the very people that could lead their peers in social revolution. Continually skimming the best off the top prevents the group from rising. Those left behind are tethered tighter.

Politics

Politics is the activities or affairs engaged in by a government, politician, or political party; the methods or tactics involved in managing a state or government. Politics affects us all. It has a profound effect on the inner city. Politics is a dirty business of favors and power wielding. Those in the hood have little power and few favors to offer. Hence there is a more negative impact on the inner city. The most striking effect politics has on inner-urban dwellers is that in this representative government the urban-impoverished are under-represented, miss-represented, or unrepresented.

Politics, like government, runs on middle class rules. Those rules are difficult for the impoverished to espouse. They seldom vote. They do not have easy access to the published records and political views of the candidates. They do not subscribe to the newspaper. They do not have convenient access to the Internet, and may not have the skills to use it. In order to read the paper or surf the Net they must visit somewhere like the local public library. They may not read well enough to understand candidate's positions, party platforms or even the ballot. They may not have convenient transportation to polling sites or council meetings. Most importantly, they do not believe that they can change fate or destiny, so why try. Many believe that elections are pre-determined anyway. Without their involvement or at least representation, politics leaps over them leaving them uninvolved and trapped in a skewed system.

Government

Government is the act or process of governing, especially the control and administration of public policy, the agency or apparatus through which a governing individual or body functions and exercises authority.

Not all government programs are negative or ineffective. Some are at least retarding inner city decline. We should be grateful for them. In fact, without them we do not know what the inner city would be like. However, they could be much more effective.

Government is huge, complicated, and confusing to the public. Most citizens don't really understand governmental structure, know which agency to contact for a given need, or understand how to obtain a prompt response. Recall that the impoverished do not plan ahead; they react only to critical needs. They do not start the search for help until the need is acute.

Government is so confusing to most urban-impoverished people that they are not able to take full advantage of it. They do not know what services are provided or where to get them. If they find the right place at the right time, the endless forms overwhelm them. They need immediate help so they frustrate quickly in a slow-moving system.

Government occasionally takes up the cause of the poor, though frequently to advance an individual's political career. Most Americans think that poverty and the issues of the inner city are someone else's problem, so the solution must come from someone else. We have abdicated such issues and their resolution to government. Local, State, and Federal Governments do the best they can to mediate or remediate what they see as inner-city problems.

Unfortunately, government defines the problems and dictates the solutions without the impoverished represented. This often either exacerbates or perpetuates the situation. Government programs usually result in enablement. Enablement is helping people enough that they can survive but not enough that they can become independent. Enablement makes and keeps them dependent. Empowerment is helping people develop the skills and systems to advance on their own. People are really helped when they learn how to help themselves. It is much more effective to find the power and assets that already exist in the inner city, validate them, and leverage them within the community. Consider the illustration commonly used to explain the difference between charity and empowerment: Give a man a fish and he will eat for a day (charity) but teach a man to fish and he will eat for a lifetime (empowerment). I disagree. I don't think teaching a man to fish is empowerment.

Empowerment is
    first, helping a man discover how to catch
        enough fish with his existing equipment to feed
        himself and his family.
    second, teaching him to acquire adequate
        equipment to not only feed himself and
        his family but to market the excess fish.
    third, training him to invest the proceeds in
        business expansion so that his business employs
        others.
    Fourth, strategizing with him to purchase the
        pond! Own a major fiscal asset.
With help they can build on their own current assets. That is real empowerment.

Some government programs take responsibility for making a dependent person independent. In doing so, the programs have just made that person dependent on them. Government does not intend to, but often becomes a shackle.

Education

Public education is government-run and private education is government-overseen. Hence, education follows middle class rules. Foreign to most inner-urban dwellers are the values that drive attendance and punctuality requirements, respect for authority, homework, work deadlines and acquiring knowledge for a better future. Without recognizing the difference in values, many schools doom inner city students to failure. Middle Class students are raised in families that value planning for the future. Impoverished students are raised in families that value only the present. Since school rules appear arbitrary and senseless to inner city students, they struggle to comply or openly rebel against them.

Some routine school procedures are ineffective for the impoverished. For example, school administrators and teachers normally communicate with parents by sending written notes and notices home with the students or sending emails or posting blogs on their web site. Inner-urban parents are not "programmed" to check daily for notes and the students do not habitually deliver the notes. Few in the hood are skilled emailers or bloggers. Many parents could not read the notes if they received them. The National Adult Literacy Survey (NALS) has published adult literacy data. Their results list five levels of literacy with Level 1 being the lowest. They determined that 43% of American adults with Level 1 literacy live in poverty. (29/ South Carolina Department of Education) Recall from chapter one that 15.3% of the US population lives in poverty. That means that 43% of the lowest literacy level exists in 15.3% of the total US population.

Burt was an obnoxious teenager who was expelled from public school twice. He was told that he needed medication to stay in control and he was never going to make it through school. He had no home; his parents had kicked him out. He slept with friends, in a city park or in an abandoned car. He had no money for medication, no one to help him, and he did not understand the requirements for receiving public assistance. He would have been a statistic; probably a fatality, if someone had not discovered him, mentored him, and empowered him to help himself. With help Burt not only graduated from High School but also College. He returned to his old hood and now helps other students do likewise.

Unless schools provide education that has immediate value for survival and methodically teach the middle class rules necessary to succeed in a middle class society, they become a fetter to the urban-impoverished.

Business and Economics

Business operates on middle class rules. These rules are foreign to the impoverished. What is obvious to people raised in the middle class is not even discernible to the impoverished. They need help internalizing these rules so that they can keep employment at a livable income. Without adopting the business protocols, they are encumbered.

Some businesses actually prey on the urban-impoverished. An extreme example is the sport shoe industry. Nike has the largest share of the market. Nike and many of its competitors reportedly outsource shoe manufacturing to third-world countries including Viet Nam and Pakistan. (30/ The Michigan Daily) No actual figures are available, but the production cost may be as low as $2 for a pair of shoes that inner city kids purchase for $100 while executives like Michael Jordan make millions and receive a complimentary lifetime supply. Whuzup with that?

The economics of the inner city were covered in chapter one. Most inner city businesses are trying to be honest, profitable businesses. Such businesses provide needed services and jobs that too often unintentionally contribute to the problem. In order to be profitable they pay low wages. To offset high security costs they charge higher prices. Lower incomes coincident with higher prices bind the poor in poverty.

Think back to the "Employment", "Income" and "Finances" sections of Chapter One. The business and economic systems constrain the urban-impoverished so that they are "stuck being poor." Only a strong impulse from outside will free them from the cycle of poverty. Absent that impulse, they are trapped.

Values

Values could be considered tethers but are not listed here because they were previously explained and are internal rather than external forces.

Media

What would you say are the dominant influences on our society? Certainly among them are movies, TV, video games, and music. Such media have more impact in the hood than in other parts of our society. That is bad news. These media may be more influential than politics, government, education, economics, and faith! Since entertainment is a daily need, poor urbanites consume more movies, TV, video games and music than anyone else. Some of these media sensationalize and validate deviate behaviors such as substance abuse and violence.

Media contends that it doesn't mold and shape culture or cause social change but rather just reflects it. Much conflicting evidence exists.

Countless news and academic articles have been written about the effect media violence has on our society. This has been an even hotter topic since the tragic Columbine, Colorado School shootings in April 1999. One such article published by Reuters Health in 2001 quotes from a report by Dr. Susan Villani a child psychiatrist at the Kennedy Krieger Institute in Baltimore Maryland. It said "adolescents who watch music videos listen to the radio and watch television movies more frequently than their peers appear to have sex at younger ages and are more likely than other adolescents to drink alcohol, smoke cigarettes and marijuana and cut class. TV violence was also associated with aggression among children as young as 4 years. While there was no evidence that violent lyrics actually caused a change in behavior, some studies indicated that listening to violent and explicit music can desensitize children to violence and promote sexual stereotyping." (31/ Reuters Health)

Where no one monitors media consumption it becomes another link in the chain restraining inner-city dwellers.

Faithlessness

The Faith described here is religious faith. It is capitalized to distinguish it from other types of faith. In the inner city Faith is manifest both internally and externally. Residents exhibit their own internal Faith or lack of Faith. Most are cynical. They have no Faith. They do not trust anyone; they rely only on themselves. They are spiritually independent. They do not think they can affect their fate. Since they do not believe they can change their destiny, in what or whom would they have Faith?

Externally the faith-based community exhibits its Faith in service to the inner city. The Faith-based community has not supported the inner city to the extent it should. The Church normally operates by middle class values and rules. It unwittingly strives to "middle-classize" inner-urban people. Some individual churches' members do more to make themselves feel good than to change the lives of those they serve. The Church is usually charitable or enabling rather than empowering. The Church too often attempts to do something for them rather than with them. Churches that use middle class mentality and methods in the inner city mute their message and bind the urban-impoverished where they are!

It would be unfair to omit acknowledging that some inner-city residents have amazingly strong Faith. Their Faith is obvious as they struggle to change their situation and circumstances. There are also a few churches and Faith-based organizations doing very effective work in inner-urban areas. Some of them are engaging the residents, discovering the existing assets, and helping the residents build on those. These Faith-based organizations are doing more to remove the fetters than any other entity.

Working with the urban-impoverished is exhausting. There are so many with critical need. It takes a lot of time and consumes a lot of emotional energy. In the next chapter let's examine how people are reacting to their struggle with these fetters.

THE FRUSTRATION - The Inner City
Exasperation   (Chapter six)

Frustration is a deep chronic sense or state of insecurity and dissatisfaction arising from unresolved problems. There are so many unresolved problems in the inner city that almost everyone involved is insecure, dissatisfied and frustrated.

Frustrated Fixers

Fixers eventually become frustrated because their efforts seem to yield little change. Most of them work very hard. It seems that they are fighting against impossible odds. The job is too big. Few understand the internal forces (values) or the external forces (fetters) in the inner city. Without understanding them no one can correctly define the problem. Sometimes fixers are battling other programs and services more than they are the problem. Government programs, non-profit services, and faith-based organizations all compete for the same funds, volunteer workers, and media attention. They even compete for clients to keep extending their string of growth years.

A good analogy for the fixers is a large unorganized group of medical workers each trying to cure the same disease. No single person can see the disease but rather each sees only one symptom. Each individual assumes that the symptom they identified is the disease. Each works desperately to eliminate that symptom. Extreme effort eventually masks or eases the symptom. It may even temporarily eliminate that symptom. Some celebrate apparent success. Meanwhile the disease continues to advance and spread; it is not eradicated or even forced into remission. Each symptom eventually reappears, often worse

75

than before. Exhausted from the work, worker frustration is inevitable.

Frustrated Residents

Inner-urban dwellers are also frustrated. They are tired of watching individuals and organizations compete for money, volunteers, publicity and them as clients. They begin to wonder what all those organizations really consider important – them, solving the problem, or just competing with each other! They long for a solution.

The impoverished see well-intentioned workers come and go. They are frustrated because they cannot leave. They are stuck, or at least think they are. Many inner-urban workers accomplish enough to get promoted out or they get frustrated and give up. I am frequently asked "how long will you be here?" It takes a long time to earn the trust of those in the hood. It took a long time to develop their skepticism and distrust; it will take at least as long to replace it with hope and trust. Just as inner-city dwellers begin to trust a fixer and make progress, that fixer leaves resulting in even more frustrated residents.

They get tired of being the subjects of experimentation. They are examined like a science project. Sometimes they hear the "solution of the month." They are seldom involved in identifying the problem or proposing a solution. They are like pawns in a game. Like the fixers, they cannot see enough of the problem to correctly state it. They appreciate any easing of the symptoms but are frequently reminded that the "disease" still exists and is still growing.

Many new programs or services are vastly over-sold. Raising funds requires promotion. It takes big plans, big expectations, and big commitments to raise big money! Too many ideas are presented as "the answer." Frustration crescendos with each subsequent promise. Meanwhile inner-urban dwellers stay poor, unhealthy, under-educated, under-employed, under-represented, under-appreciated, and ever more frustrated.

Frustrated Politicians and Government Workers

Politicians and government workers are frustrated because the hood's problems are constantly a monkey on their back. Neither Democrats nor Republicans have shown the ability to make a lasting inner-urban difference. Bureaucrats are weary from constant pressure to solve the problem. They believe that the only hope is legislative change, funds allocation or some other governmental action. If only the hood would just go away their lives would be much more enjoyable.

Frustrated Churches

The Church is frustrated. Congregations believe that they have provided bountiful funds and volunteers. In spite of all they have done for the urban-impoverished they see little improvement. Few churches have ministered in the hood but many have donated funds to the Para-church organizations that do. They think their "sacrificial assistance" should be more effective.

Frustrated Suburbanites

Suburbanites are frustrated because they do not understand the problem. They assume that it is a simple problem with a simple solution. They wonder, "Why don't they just stop it?" "Why doesn't someone solve the problem?" Actually, most individuals in the suburbs only think about the hood after a sensational news report. When violence spills out of the hood or when the huge costs of social programs are highlighted, they are upset.

Frustration has led us all to blame each other. Who among us is affected by this problem? Who is to blame for the condition of the hood? Are the residents of the hood or banks or grocery stores or City Government or Federal Government or social services or the suburbanites who fled or the Church or the school system or corporations or society in general? Is anyone to blame? Are we all to blame? We've blamed each other but that has not changed the outcome.

A better question is who or what can fix it? The answer to this question is not obvious. Who really is responsible to solve this problem? Let's answer some of these questions in the next chapter.

PART FOUR: TOGETHER WE CAN CHANGE IT

The biggest military project the world has ever seen was the World War II Normandy Invasion. The biggest engineering project ever accomplished was the Apollo Moon Project. The biggest medical problem ever solved was not a cure for a disease; it was mapping the human genome, the Human Genome Project. That project required countless persons in many organizations working in harmony to accomplish the task. The project took thirteen years to complete. The U.S. Department of Energy and the National Institutes of Health coordinated it. Wellcome Trust from the United Kingdom was a major partner. China, France, Germany, and Japan were significant contributors. (32/ Oak Ridge National Laboratory) There were many other countries involved. Solving the inner city problem will likely take similar manpower, similar cooperation, similar leadership, and similar ingenuity. If we do not solve it, like a sinking ship, it will eventually suck us under with it!

THE FELLOWSHIP – Those Affected by the Inner City (Chapter seven)

Fellowship is the condition of sharing similar interests, ideals, or experiences. Fellowship has been described as several "fellows" in the same "ship." These fellows must have a common objective and work closely with each other to endure the storms and arrive at the destination. We are all impacted by the inner city. Therefore we are all be part of the fellowship. No one is immune to inner-urban issues. The problems are constantly becoming more complex and affecting more people.

Should you really care about the inner city? You better care! Here are a few are reasons that will likely resonate with you.

Money

It should now be obvious that many of your tax dollars are being spent to
1) provide support for those who do not work,
2) provide healthcare for those who have no health insurance,
3) provide law enforcement to control violence or at least contain it, and
4) deal with the results of alcohol and drug abuse.

Total welfare spending is a staggering amount - $786.6 billion in 2010 with about 64% from the Federal Government, 26% from various State Governments and the remaining 10% from local governments. (33/ US Government Spending) That makes welfare about 13% of federal spending! These are such huge numbers that they are difficult to grasp. To better understand the magnitude in 2010 welfare spending I calculated the average amount per tax return. Per efile.com the total number of tax returns in

2010 was 141,536,000. (34/ efile.com) Dividing $786,600,000,000 by 141,536,000 yields $5,558 from every return. Some of these may represent two joint tax payers. To those with large incomes who pay large tax bills this will be surprisingly low and is likely less than their share. To those with less income and small tax bills this will be shockingly high and likely more than their share.

The rate of increase in welfare spending from 1991 to 2000 was 7.5% per year (35/ The Heritage Foundation, page 5) and from 2001 to 2010 the rate of increase was 21% per year. (36/ US Government Spending 2) You tax payers pay more welfare every year.

I also calculated the 2010 cost of welfare per poor person by dividing $786.6 billion spent by the previously stated 46,215,956 impoverished persons yielding $17,020 each. Not all impoverished people are inner-city residents. Remember we estimated in chapter one about three-fourths of them are. Regardless of where they live, those below the poverty line cost tax payers $17,020 per year in 2010.

Welfare spending fluctuates as the Executive Branch and the two Houses of Congress change. Recently it has vastly increased. It should also be stated that the housing market collapse that resulted in near financial collapse has severely dampened our economy.

These costs are actually understated unless all the overhead is included. Idea House wrote, "Seldom considered are the costs and expenses incurred by huge bureaucratic networks supposedly created to meet children's needs . . . ." (28/ Idea House, Page 5)

Some would like to cease these tax funded programs and services. However, ending these would only suspend the cost for a season. In time, after the situation further deteriorated, we would be spending more than we do now to correct the ever-expanding problem. We cannot do that anyway. Society has a responsibility for those less fortunate.

Physical safety

It should be evident that our loved-ones are all at risk of being harmed during a violent crime. Well, isn't this an isolated problem, an inner city problem? Are they not just killing each other? It does not really affect very many, does it? No, it doesn't. Only occasionally is someone from outside the hood injured; usually because they just happen to be present when a crime is committed - a random victim, a witness or an unlucky by-stander. The most often injured outsiders are Police officers who are injured or killed responding to a crime.

Every time inner city crime spills over into the suburbs there is an outcry. A frequent comment is "I never thought it would happen here!" Guess what, with inattention and enough time, it <u>will</u> happen near you.

The youth crime problem is a great example. Several years ago the youth crime problem was predominantly an inner city problem. It has expanded. Today urban crime is not very newsy. When a kid from one of our better neighborhoods or some high profile adult's child is a crime victim, that's big news! Remember the Columbine High School massacre? That awakened the nation! On April 20, 1999 two students of Columbine High School in an upscale Denver suburb killed twelve and injured twenty-four fellow students, killed one staff member, and killed themselves in the worst school massacre in American history. It is still the worst massacre in a North American secondary school. Columbine wasn't the first school shooting and unfortunately it wasn't the last. It was so shocking because so many students from an upper middle class neighborhood were injured or killed. I'm not suggesting that someone from the inner city participated in the massacre or even that school massacres began in urban impoverished American schools. I am, however, stating that youth violence began in the inner city and radiated out from there.

By the way, what will it take for some of us to become enraged about inner city youth homicides? How many inner-urban young people are we willing to see killed? What is the number? When is it no longer tolerable?

All the highest youth homicide rates in America are in impoverished areas – most in inner cities. Realize that for every fatality there is a family which is often quite large. Also realize that the whole neighborhood is traumatized. Even if it was just an inner city problem, these are not just numbers. These are young people. Are not inner-city people just as valuable as anyone else? Yes, of course they are. Whose son or daughter's death will stir us to action? These are not just statistics! These are people, young people!

Cultural Development

It is not apparent to all that cultural change is flowing outward from the inner city! Where do you think social change originates? Most people answer, in the suburbs or in the middle class. After all, aren't they the movers and shakers? Yes, but social change, or at least some social change starts in the inner city and radiates outward.

Consider some of the recent changes in American society. Take music, for instance. Hip-hop and rap have pervaded the music scene. They both came through the inner city. According to National Geographic their roots are in Africa in the sixteen-hundreds. (37/ National Geographic, page 108) Slaves brought them to America. Hip-hop resurfaced in Harlem and South Bronx, New York in the 1970s. (37/ National Geographic, page 105) Suburbanites thought it would not have appeal outside the hood. Guess what. It does. It now has world-wide appeal; the second largest market is France. (37/ National Geographic, page 115)

Clothing fads have recently come from the inner city. Take for example, young males with the low-rider britches. You know, boys wearing their jeans half way down their buttocks with underwear on display. Suburban parents did not expect to ever see that in their area. Surprise! That also came first from the penal system to the inner city then to other areas.

Body art is now seen in nearly every neighborhood. You've seen the tattoos and piercings. Yep, that came from the prisons where inmates had little but decorating themselves to occupy their time. It branched out to the inner city and then to other parts of American society.

Substance abuse has invaded every class and nearly every neighborhood in America. Substance abuse was first epidemic in inner-urban neighborhoods.

Our Americanized-English language is continually being peppered with slang. Listen to your kids or friends and realize how much of their lingo originated in the hood. Most of that slang comes from the urban-impoverished. You may have recognized some of the slang in previous chapters. If you did not, wait a few months. You will.

I could go on but if you are not convinced yet, I won't be the one to convince you. As I alleged in the introduction, the inner city really is an emerging culture.

I hope you agree that all of us "fellows" are in this ship together. We need to work together. The first step is the hardest. Where do we start? That is the next subject.

THE FOUNDATION - The Inner City Hope
(Chapter eight)

A foundation is the strongest part of a structure, a base upon which other parts rest or are overlaid and supported. The root problem in the inner city is neither lack of money nor lack of services nor lack of education nor lack of jobs nor lack of intelligence. It is not the restraints on residents or even their values. It is lack of foundation! The major obstacle for the residents, and a major frustration for those who try to help them, is that everything they build soon crumbles. There is nothing firm on which to build in impoverished urban America.

No structure is secure without a good foundation. Engineers have developed different types of foundations for various applications. They are all designed according to precise physical laws. Every structure must rest on an adequate support. Big, heavy buildings are structurally connected to bedrock, a firm layer of natural rock beneath the soil's surface. No matter what a person builds, it will crumble without a proper foundation.

As you read chapters one and two many of you wondered where to start to fix this complex problem. Just like constructing a building, you start with the foundation. There is only one rock-solid foundation, Faith in God. Faith is the only foundation that will support the structures that must be built in order to change the inner city. However, faith in a falsehood is useless, moveable and non-supportive. A person can have faith, I mean really believe, that fire will not burn them. When they put their hand in the fire that faith will not prevent them from being burned! In the same way, faith in anything or anyone other than the God of creation will fail. Reality exists apart from believers and non-believers. God is who He says He is, whether we believe it or not. Denying the truth certainly does not change or even diminish it. Reality is not the way we think things are or how we wish things were; it is how things really are!

While an engineering student at university I took a Philosophy class. The class was mostly about existentialism. We talked about whether we could know that we really existed and if we could be sure that anyone or anything existed. We repeatedly heard the argument that everything that wasn't us may just be in our imagination. That is an interesting thought. However, I was stunned to observe that every class started and ended the same way. All students arrived at approximately the same time, came in through one of the doors, walked down an aisle, sat in a chair, and listened for fifty minutes. They then stood up, gathered their books, walked back up the aisle and left through one of the doors. No one just disappeared or walked through the wall or levitated through the ceiling or transformed into a ball of green goo. I even tried to imagine that they had, but couldn't make myself believe it! Try as I did I could not change reality with my imagination.

Many of you will think that I have over-simplified the situation in stating that the most essential need is Faith. My time in the inner city has totally convinced me that approaching God through faith in Christ Jesus is the only hope. It is obvious to Christians that faith in God is the only spiritual hope. It is not as obvious, but equally true that faith in God is the only hope physically, economically, socially, mentally and every "other-ly." Health, economy, culture and knowledge need a good foundation. In the same way programs and services can only stand on a firm foundation. I acknowledge that we can and have made temporary improvement in some aspects of the hood.

Permanent change requires more. Try to make lasting improvement in the health and well-being of inner city people. You'll fail because there is no foundation. Try to build a good economy in the hood. It will crumble because there is no foundation. Try to build a better social structure in an inner-urban area. It will fall because there is no foundation. Try to educate the impoverished. You will fail without first building a good foundation. Try to build anything good in the inner city and it will disintegrate because there is no foundation.

Even values require a good foundation. Try to change the values of the residents of the hood and you will fail unless you first bring them to Faith. After all, what determines values? Our beliefs determine our values.

The classic example of a magnificent building on an inadequate foundation is the Tower of Pisa. The tower of Pisa is not new; it was begun in August 1173. The building structure is quite strong but it has been listing more and more since the date of its completion. It began to lean immediately. As the lean became visibly obvious it became a tourist attraction. Italians were concerned that it would eventually lean past its center of gravity, fall over and collapse. In 1990 the tower was closed so that twelve years of corrective construction could be completed. They didn't right the building but rather modified its foundation; supported and halted the lean such that it still attracts visitors.

What from the Tower of Pisa applies to the inner city? First, like any structure, nothing built into the impoverished will stand without a good foundation. Second, bad foundations can be corrected with careful planning and hard work.

The only foundation that will support what we need to build is Faith in God. God created heaven and earth, including everything in them. Since that is true, it is true that He created the inner city and He created faith. You may be thinking "then He really messed up!" No, we messed up what He created! We are stewards of what He created. We have not stewarded some of His creation very well. God created the hood. Only He can change what it has become.

As I drove home from a "Stop the Violence" Town Hall Meeting one night I reflected on what I had just heard. Mentally sorting through nearly two and a half hours of conversation, I was nagged by a question, "what is the real problem?" Reflecting on each successive speaker I thought, "The root problem is sin." God gave us the definition of sin in the Bible. Sin is any action that does not spring from our faith in Him. It is acting in ways contrary to His nature and His instructions. This conclusion was so obvious. I am not saying people who live in the hood are sinners as opposed to suburbanites who aren't. Nor am I saying that those in the inner city sin bigger sins or sin more often than others. The problem is we all sin; we have not responded to these circumstances in a Godly way. Now I know that this is not such a profound thought. I also know that we could keep reducing the real problem past sin to man's sinful nature then to evil then to demons then to Satan. I agree with all of these but choose to just call it a sin problem.

Sin is a spiritual problem. Spiritual problems require spiritual solutions. Only God can provide spiritual solutions. He has already provided the solution and communicated it in the Bible. The solution is submission to God through Jesus His son.

One of the ministries with which I served operated a

small business that employed the urban-impoverished. Those who never came to faith in Christ did not make the changes necessary to break their fetters. Some tried to fake it. They claimed they had Faith in God but their actions invalidated that claim. They were never able to really change their habits or environment. Those who really came to Faith began to change their values, change their lives and break their fetters. They became good employees, good spouses, good parents, and good citizens. For some the transition was rapid and for others it was slow. They went spiritually from independence to dependence and socially from dependence to independence.

Most people who are working to help those in the inner city are striving to bring the residents from social dependence to independence. That's trying to land the plane before it takes off. We must first take them from spiritual independence to dependence on God. That's foundational. Only then can they become socially independent.

I don't claim that only those trusting in God can break the inner city shackles or deny that exceptions exist. I do bear witness that nearly all of the impoverished that permanently break their fetters are believers. I am also not saying that all who believe in God will change their values, but a very high percentage will.

Suppose we agree that faith in God is the only firm foundation. How do we get it? Do we get it by meditation for hours, or by in-depth study, or by sacrificial service? No. Do we get it by donating large sums of money or by agonizing over what's wrong? No. We do not come to faith in God by doing good things. We rather do good things because we have faith in God and want to obey Him. God does not allow us to determine what Faith is or how we get it. After all, God created Faith and the way to get it. He left the instructions for us in the Bible. He says that we come to Faith in Him by placing our Faith in Jesus. Faith in Jesus is a life changing, even controlling, belief that Jesus is who He says He is, He did what He says He did, and it means what He says it means. It is a decision, a decision to admit that there is a God and he is not you, or me. It's a decision to place ourselves under the authority of the God of creation through Jesus, the Son of God. Jesus paid the price for our sin on the cross at Calvary. As the songwriter expressed it, "I owed a debt I could not pay. He paid a debt He did not owe." It is a decision to accept the payment Jesus made and to live to serve Him the rest of our days.

The result of such Faith is not a care-free problem-less life, but rather is a purposeful life with the strength and companionship to survive whatever comes. Now that's a foundation! Nothing can destroy those who are firmly trusting in the one who created foundations.

Are there no other ways to come to God? No. He said there are not. He should know.

Those who trust in Him will be able to survive whatever comes their way here on earth. Then, when they leave this earth in death they will join Him in heaven for eternity.

What a deal! If you can find a better deal, take it! Until then, ponder what I've said. It's worth considering. It's worth trying. It's worth whatever it takes!

Once the foundation is laid we can build on it. What should we build? How do we build it? Who's going to lead? Let's discuss these next.

PART FIVE: ONLY THE CHURCH CAN LEAD –
WHERE TO START AND WHAT TO DO

You can lead a horse to water but you can't make him drink. Unknown author

Lead, follow, or get out of the way. Unknown author

One spring I was picked to be on a jury for a criminal trial, it was my third criminal jury. Like the other two it was a long, frustrating and stressful trial. After testimony ended and closing statements were delivered, we were given the case to deliberate and reach a verdict.

Our first duty was to select a Foreman. As in the two previous cases, the selection wasn't easy. The most experienced and best skilled do not necessarily want to serve. Someone else, for whatever reason, typically wants to lead. Such was the case on this day.

The first two hours of our time were spent accomplishing little. Various jurors were drawing preliminary opinions and entrenching in them. It appeared that a verdict would be difficult to reach. Then suddenly a fortunate event happened, a person with superior leadership skills and judicial experience began to subtly lead in a way that was so supportive of the foreman that few, if any other jurors, were aware. This juror skillfully and respectfully guided discussion so that all jurors were heard and a verdict was reached within minutes. What difference good leadership made!

Since the root problem is spiritual only God can solve it. God is the only capable leader. "Oh, get real" some say, "how can that happen?" For such a time as this God has chosen the Church as His agent on earth. The Church is God's earthly leader. Only the Church can lead us to solve the problems.

THE FORMULA - The Inner City Solution
(Chapter nine)

There are no quick fixes, no Shake 'n Bake (an easy fried food simulating product introduced by General Foods in the mid-1960s) solutions. This situation developed over decades and may take decades to remediate. The resources required are a corps of people, funds, plans, and facilities. But it takes more than that; we've had those for years and have not made much progress! It takes planning, coordination and commitment to stick with it until success is achieved.

Values must be changed and fetters must be broken. These cannot all be done simultaneously so we must first attack the most constraining ones.

Revaluing

Driving Force

Once those in the inner-city have come to Faith they will be able to replace survival as their driving force. No other value is likely to change until they are freed from the constant struggle to make it through today. Survival pressure must be decreased enough for residents to focus on tomorrow and beyond.

I don't advocate trying to make them Middle Class. The importance of not imposing our will and values on them cannot be over emphasized. The residents of the hood must develop their own new driving force. Asked to suggest one, I offer improvement. We must empower them to get involved in their own improvement. People don't consciously choose their driving force; it is the result of the foundation on which they build. With good discipleship their Faith will found a driving force that leads to their improvement.

World View

The urban-impoverished must be freed to explore outside the boundaries of their neighborhood so that they have a chance to broaden their worldview. We must invite them to be our guests at our suburban church services and visit theirs as well. We must go with them to sporting events, universities, theaters, museums and government offices. We need to help them develop the desire and infrastructure to take their peers to such places. Together we must create ways for them to travel to other cities, states and nations.

New experiences will broaden their perspective and world view.

Destiny

As they grow in their Faith they will learn to change their destiny; fate does not control them but rather they control their fate. We must help them learn to identify alternatives but let them make choices. Afterward we can help them evaluate the results of their decisions and consider the likely outcomes of other possible choices.

We should together study the Scripture passages that teach us how to control ourselves and our future.

Social Emphasis

We must include them in society. Interaction need not always be at our urging but since someone must start building the relationships, let us be first. Once we all acknowledge each other's worth, we can work together to help them become self-sufficient. Self-sufficiency will be the target but they must identify intermediate steps and milestones. They won't become self-sufficient until they want to and learn how. We can't impose it on them.

Middle-classers describe their actions as common sense. I think that common sense is either miss-named or overstated. This sense is only common to those who have lived it for a time. Self-sufficiency is learned and developed over time. Many years may be required for some to gain the skills.

Family Structure

We should not try to force them to become Patriarchal but rather help them strengthen their family units. Families must be reinforced so that they develop strong men with proper respect for women and families. Young men need to learn Biblical character including Godly manhood and Godly fatherhood.

It Takes a Village (by Hillary Rodham Clinton) <u>and</u> *It Takes a Family* (by Rick Santorum) to raise a child. It also will take a village and a family to change our society. At the 2005 Christian Community Development Association Conference John Perkins, a well-respected long-time inner-city social soldier, said, "The real problem with the hood is the breakdown of the family!" Unless we help rebuild the family, our labor will be in vain.

Most will agree that the American family has atrophied and is in danger of disintegrating. The most extreme example of lost family structure is in the inner city. Reflect back to previous descriptions of urban-impoverished families. Few inner city children are raised with their father involved in their lives. Single teenage mothers raise many: immature "children" are raising their own children. Indianapolis Juvenile Court Judge Marilyn Moore said that the biggest problem in the hood is that "there are too many children trying to raise children!"

Time

As Faith matures those in the hood will more highly value the future. Christianity teaches sacrifice today for blessing tomorrow.

Time management skills are learned; not endowed. We need to help them understand that most systems in America operate on middle class rules that are rooted in middle class values. They needn't become Middle Class but must follow these rules in order to improve their circumstances.

Money

Like time, money's value to the urban-impoverished will change. Money management skills are also acquired so we must help them develop them.

Removing Fetters

Education

Similar to time and money, new value will be assigned to education. Educators should consistently a) make lessons relevant to today's needs and b) impress students with the future value of knowledge and skill.

The middle class values and rules necessary for success will best be validated and taught in schools at the same time they are being reinforced in other societal interactions. Involving certain urban impoverished persons as teachers or teacher-assistants may facilitate the learning.

Politics

The most important political change is proper representation - assuring that the residents of the inner cities are adequately represented. That will likely accomplished as they elect their own representatives to various government bodies.

Business and Economics

More businesses must be lured to the inner city by emphasizing its advantages such as the concentration of residents. The demographics offer more potential than the typical owner realizes.

Businesses must be encouraged to pay livable wages and offer basic fringe benefits.

Media

Ok, let's get real. Media does affect society. This is a delicate issue because we believe in the right to free speech. Let's not tread on that but instead find ways to encourage less destructive media production and use.

Government Programs and Services

Government programs and services must be modified to really empower residents of the hood. The first and most effective step is to involve them in the design of such programs and services. They will benefit by learning planning skills. Government will benefit from their experience and perspective such that real problems will be identified and effective solutions implemented.

Government needs to stop taking responsibility for impoverished urban residents and their problems. Helping them find their own solutions and holding them accountable will produce far better results.

Wouldn't it benefit to hire some from the inner city to design and administer modified programs and services?

A new approach may help. Working together to access the assets that now exist in the hood and leveraging those will meet less resistance than looking for root problems to solve. George E. Reed of the U.S. Army War College wrote "today's solutions become tomorrow's problems." Are our former solutions some of the current problems? Probably. Let's find what is working now so we can bolster and amplify it.

Governmental rules and forms need to be adapted to the language skills of those served.

Politicians and bureaucrats must be held accountable for real results not just continually serving more people.

Encouraging staff members to live in the hood and hiring a few staff from current residents will help understand the residents and identify current assets.

Private Nonprofit Organizations

Private nonprofit organizations also need to modify their methods. Time and effort spent to develop collaborations and eliminate overlaps will yield more efficient use of funds and other resources.

Encouraging staff members to live in the hood and hiring a few staff from current residents will help understand the residents and identify current assets.

Like government agencies, NPOs need to involve the

residents, stop taking responsibility for them and their problems, find and leverage current inner city assets and be held responsible for results not just continually serving more people.

Unfortunately I do not know how to do all these. I do, however know, that together we can and we must learn.

New Approach

These all require more than effort and determination! We need a new approach, a new formula. A formula is a recipe, prescription, set form, or method. The formula presented here is not detailed enough to be called a recipe. This formula is a methodology. The formula for the hood is fellowship, cooperation, participation, persistence, and faith. Many develop cute acrostics to help us remember. I crafted my own: FAITH. The letters stand for: Family, Association, Integration, Tenacity, and Hope.

Fellowship

In order to change the hood we must be and act like a family. We must all realize we are part of this "fellowship" of mankind. All of us are affected, all of us are involved and all our efforts will be required to change the situation. No one is exempt. Unless all of society participates in solving the problem, it will not be solved.

We cannot continue to allow a portion of our society to be chained in poverty. It's not fair to them and it is a drag on us all. We cannot just throw money at the problem by paying taxes and abdicating the problem and its solution to government. Neither can we relegate the problem and solution to nonprofit organizations. We have done that. It didn't work! All of society contributes to the problem so all of society must participate in its solution.

Together we must find ways to empower poor urbanites with the habits and skills to obtain and maintain employment at livable wages. Working for less than the FCSUM is not fair to anyone. Working together we can recruit cost effective businesses such as grocery stores and banks to the inner city.

Association

The problem in the inner city is so complex that it is futile for any organization or program to function in isolation. We cannot solve the problems, or even find the root problems without cooperation. Cooperation is more than acknowledging each other. It is investigating together, evaluating together, planning together, and solving together. Cooperating with others may even make the task enjoyable. I realize that all will not have the same motivation. In fact, some may not appear to be compatible with others but we can all unite against the enemy – generational poverty. With common cause we will find a common approach. Only then is solution possible. Competition and strife will disappear as we co-labor.

We need to be like one huge group of medical workers all coordinated and cooperating in one effort to identify the real disease and cure it. Teamwork produces better results. Teamwork takes selfless effort. On a real team there are no heroes and no zeros! This is no place to advance political aspirations or maintain bureaucratic thinking. Non-profit organizations must stop competing with each other.

Integration

No real solution can be identified or implemented

without the intimate involvement of the urban-impoverished. No one can solve the problem for them. They must be involved in every step. They must identify the symptoms, isolate the root problems, propose solutions, draft methods, and implement the solutions. With their involvement will come vesting in the solutions and the outcomes. By the way, their involvement is the first step toward their empowerment.

Lines of communication must be short and rapid. Government-like complication will retard advancement. During the 1990's Corporate America developed ways to move information faster and make better decisions closer to the issues. Those techniques will help prevent confusion and avoid the paralyzing duplication of efforts. Government and city schools will need to be user-friendlier by adapting to the differences in value systems.

A new focus is needed. Rather than looking for what is missing in the inner city, we need to find what is good in the inner city. We must identify the current assets, validate them, strengthen them, and leverage them. The assets will be different in various inner cities. Every inner city has strengths. We must find them and use them to the neighborhood's advantage.

Examples of indigenous assets are:
1. In one neighborhood a resident Pastor has a burden and a gift for enlisting mature men to mentor young men.
2. In another neighborhood a schoolteacher is impassioned make every lesson relevant to both survival and building for the future.
3. In a given neighborhood a local business has fought the trend to move to the suburbs, feels strongly about hiring local residents, and teaches them good

working habits.
4. A group of firefighters has developed a popular, effective summer day camp for residents in another neighborhood.
5. A professional athlete returns to his roots each off-season to mentor kids and instill ambition.

These are just examples. How can assets such as these be used for the good of all? The objective is to find all the positive attributes of a given neighborhood, celebrate them, help strengthen them, build on them, and leverage them to benefit all.

The impoverished are intelligent but need help structuring their thoughts. They know best what they need. Our methods must better embrace impoverished class values. We must spend time with them, listen to them, and learn from them. If you do not think that you can learn from the urban impoverished, they probably will not learn much from you either!

Tenacity

It will take constant, consistent attention for a long time to realize lasting results. A way to achieve success is to identify the individuals living in the hood who are burdened to stay there through good and bad times, those driven to change it. Those in the hood are the most heavily invested and most able to effect change.

Even when we work as an organized, integrated team it will be a long hard battle. We must stay committed and stay focused. Without persistence we will fail.

Former United States President Calvin Coolidge highlighted the value of persistence by saying, "Nothing in the world can occupy the place of persistence. Talent does not . . . nothing is more common than a person with talent but without success. Intelligence will not . . . genius without remuneration (is) almost a proverb. Education by itself is not enough either; the world is full of educated twits."

Hope

Our hope cannot be a wish or desire. It must be a conviction grounded in reality. Our hope must conform to the archaic definition: confidence, trust, or faith. Faith is the only firm foundation. The inner city problem is a spiritual problem that can only have a spiritual solution. Only God can solve this problem. He normally works through people.

God's instrument in the world is the Church. Only the Church can lead this effort. The Church should work with government, nonprofit organizations, individuals and businesses. We need everyone's help. The Church is not currently leading or even considering this to be its problem to solve.

It's time for the Church, the living body of Christ, to do what Jesus did. Jesus said in Luke 4:18 "The Spirit of the Lord is on me, because he has anointed me to preach good news to the poor. He has sent me to proclaim freedom for the prisoners and recovery of sight for the blind, to release the oppressed . . . . [NIV] (38/ The Holy Bible) Believers, having been anointed to be like Him, should do likewise. Some local churches and individual Christians are at the forefront of this battle but, where is the Church, the united body of believers? It's time for all church bodies to unite as the Church and minister together as it was anointed to!

The Church needs to be servant leaders. The members need to come motivated to empower the impoverished to help themselves.

When Helping Hurts by Steve Corbett and Brian Fikkert is one of the best books on the harm caused by socially minded people, including Christians, doing what they think needs to be done. Read it; no study it.

The Church must stop making itself feel good by going to the inner city for a few days to do something for the people there. The Church can only help by being involved relationally for long enough to serve with the urban-impoverished as Christ did. My friend Joel Freeman, PhD said this, "the Church's major emphasis must be relationships and flexibility." Prior to tripping to the inner city the Church should take time to evaluate and adjust its motives. A season of prayer and attitudinal adjustment is the best preparation.

Who would describe the hood as a joyful place? No one that I know would. Joy is scarce in the inner city. "And now these three remain: faith, hope and love. But the greatest of these is love." 1 Corinthians 13:13 (38/ The Holy Bible) Without faith hope cannot exist. Without hope love cannot exist. And without love joy is absent. Faith is the beginning of the path to joy.

Even Church leadership will not assure success. Even the Church cannot do it, only God can! God said in 2 Chronicles 7:14 "if my people, who are called by my name, will humble themselves and pray and seek my face and turn from their wicked ways, then will I hear from heaven and will forgive their sin and will heal their land." [NIV] (38/ The Holy Bible) The Church must first humble itself (admit that we have not solved the problem and we cannot solve the problem) then pray, seek God's will, and turn from its wicked ways. Only then we can expect God to forgive our sin and heal the inner city.

So, Church, LEAD us to

Fellowship – everyone, join in the struggle for a solution,

Associate - organize, plan, and work together,

Integrate inner city dwellers and suburbanites

Tenaciously - team together to persistently pursue completion, unwilling to quit

Hope – pray and trust God to redeem the poor, free the captives restore sight to the blind and release the oppressed

Parting Plea: What Now?

Through the years I have trained myself to show little emotion. I am focused to a fault. In spite of the popularity of on-line poker and events like the World Series of Poker, I am not a poker player or have any desire to become one. I have, however, spent years developing a poker face and demeanor.

Few events or situations squeeze my emotions to the surface but when I reflect on experiences with those in the hood I am moved. Their life is so stressful. I remember a time when I broke down emotionally. No, it wasn't in the trenches. It happened when I was away from the inner city in the security of a middle class home in a middle class suburb. A compassionate friend saw my distress and put a warm towel on my neck to comfort me. Pent up emotions spewed to the surface as I sobbed. On the front line of this battle I dared not break character long enough to relax. But here I let it go. I realized that the urban impoverished can't ever get far enough away for long enough to release their emotions. For them the emotional pressure is constant.

Now what? I often ask myself, now what? What would God have me do based on what He has shown me? What should you do based on what He has shown you? Will you help? Will you beseech God to show you the role He wants you to play? He has a role for you. In case you respond, "I'm not trained or equipped." Let me quote someone else, "God doesn't call the equipped, He rather equips the called."

James 1:23 & 24 says "For if anyone is a hearer of the word and not a doer, he is like a man who looks at his natural face in a mirror; for once he has looked at himself and gone away, he has immediately forgotten what kind of person he was." This has been more than an intellectual exercise for me. I hope it also has for you. Let this book be a mirror to check yourself.

In Luke 4:18 & 19 Jesus is quoted saying, "the spirit of the Lord is upon me, because He anointed me to preach the gospel to the poor. He has sent me to proclaim release to the captives, and recovery of sight to the blind, to set free those who are oppressed, to proclaim the favorable year of the Lord." Only He can do all of these. He is using Christ-followers, His ambassadors, to change the world.

Join me, please.

Works Cited

1/ US Census Bureau (2010). S1702. *Poverty Status in the Past 12 Months of families,* Washington, DC, Census 2010, http://factfinder2.census.gov/

2/ US Census Bureau (2010). S1701. *Poverty Status in the Past 12 Months,* Washington, DC, Census 2010, http://factfinder2.census.gov/

3/ US Census Bureau (2000). *GCT-H1. Total and Occupied Housing Units for Urban/Rural and Metropolitan Population: 2000, Washington, DC,* Census 2000 Summary File 1 (SF 1), http://factfinder.census.gov/

4/ Proctor, Bernadette D. and Joseph Dalaker (September 2003). Table A1, *Poverty Status of People by Family Relationship, Race, and Hispanic Origin: 1959 to 2002,* Washington, DC, Poverty in the United States: 2002, US Census Bureau

5/ US Census Bureau (2005). Figure 3. *Number in Poverty and Poverty Rate: 1959 to 2004,* Washington, DC, www.census.gov/hhes/poverty/poverty04/pov 04fig03

6/ US Census Bureau (2010). B25008. *Total Population in Occupied Housing Units by Tenure,* Washington, DC, Census 2010, http://factfinder2.census.gov/

7/ O'Neill, Rebecca (September 2002). *Experiments in Living: The Fatherless Family,* CIVITAS (the Institute for the Study of Civil Society), London, England

8/ US Department of Justice, Federal Bureau of Investigation. Crimes and Crime Rates by Type and Geographic Community: 2009, Table 307. *Washington, DC,* www2.fbi.gov/ucr/cius2009/index.html

9/ Gallup, *Most Americans Believe Crime in U.S. Is Worsening,* Washington, DC, www.gallup.com/poll/150464/americans-believe-crime-worsening.aspx?version=print

10/ Anyon, J. (1995). *Race, Social Class, and Educational Reform in an Inner-city School.* New York, NY, Teachers College Record, volume 97, Number 1, Columbia

University

11/ National Center for Education Statistics (2010). *Summary Table of High School Dropouts, Completions, and Graduation Rates, Table A-1,* Washington, DC, nces.ed.gov

12/ National Center for Education Statistics (2010). *Public High School Graduation Rates, Indicator 32,* Washington, DC, nces.ed.gov

13/ National Center for Education Statistics (2010). *Event dropout rates and number and distribution of 15- through 24-year-olds who dropped out of grades 10-12, by selected characteristics: October 2008,* , Washington, DC, nces.ed.gov

14/ USA Today, *Big-city schools struggle with graduation rates, 6/20/2006.* McLean, VA, www.usatoday.com

15/ Buy Here Pay Here. *Buy Here Pay Here Interest Rates, 9/7/12.* www.buyingcarswithbadcredit.com/buy-here-pay-here-interest-rates

16/ US Department of Labor. *Minimum Wage,* Washington, DC, http://dol.gov/dol/topic/wages/minimumwage.html

17/ Labor Law Center. *State Minimum Wage,* Garden Grove, CA, www.laborlawcenter.comt-State-Minimum-Wage-Rates.aspx

18/ US Department of Commerce. *State and County QuickFacts,* Washington, DC, http://quickfacts.census.gov/qfd/states/00000.html

19/ US Department of Health & Human Services. 2012 HHS Poverty Guidelines, Washington, DC, http://aspe.hhs.gov/poverty/12poverty.shtml

20/ National Academy of Sciences. Tow-Adult-Two-Child Poverty Thresholds: 2009 and 2010, Washington, DC www.bls.gov/pir/spm/spm_threshold_200910.xls

21/ Consumer Federation of America. *Cashed Out: Consumers Pay Steep Premium to "Bank" at Check Cashing Outlets,* Washington, DC, www.consumerfed.org

22/ Mittal, Anuradha (December 2004). *Going Hungry in America,* Oakland, CA: Alternet, Oakland Institute

23/ US Census Bureau (2004). *Table 7. People With or Without Health Insurance Coverage by Selected Characteristics: 2003 and 2004,* Washington, DC, www.census.gov/hhes/www/hlthins/hlthin04

24/ Payne, Ruby K., PhD (2003). *A Framework for Understanding Poverty,* HO 10 & 11, Highlands, TX: aha! Process, Inc.

25/ Payne, Ruby K., PhD, Philip DeVol, and Terie Dreussi

Smith (2001). *Bridges Out of Poverty,* Highlands, TX: aha! Process, Inc.

26/ Community Service. *St. Louis Non-Profit Agencies, Community Service Office,* Washington University in St. Louis, Saint Louis, MO, www.communityservice.wustl.edu/stlagencies/dispoay.php

27/ Washington University. *Social Work and Social Web Sites, Washington University in St. Louis,* St. Louis, MO, http://gwbwebwustl.edu/resources/Pages/socialservicesresourcesintro.aspx

28/ Idea House (2001). National Center for Policy Analysis, Dallas, TX, www.ncpa.org/pi/welfare/!wel15.htm

29/ South Carolina Department of Education (2006). *The State of Literacy in America: Estimates at the Local, State, and National Levels,* Columbia, SC, www.sclrc.org/NalsNarrative

30/ The Michigan Daily (September 1997). The University of Michigan, Anarbor, MI, www.pub.umich.edu/1997/sep/09-11-97

31/ Reuters Health (2001). *Research links media to children's aggression,* New York, NY

32/ Oak Ridge National Laboratory (2005). *Human Genome Project Information,* Oak Ridge, TN, www.ornl.gov/sci/techresources/Human_Genome

33/ US Government Spending. *United States Federal State and Local Government Spending Fiscal Year 2010 I $ billion,* www.usgovernmentspending.com/usgs_print.php

34/ efile.com. *Almost 80% of All U.S. Taxpayers efiled Income Tax Returns in 2011,* Fairfax, VA, www.efile.com/efile-tax-return-direct-deposit-statistics/

35/ The Heritage Foundation (2001). The Size and Scope of Means-Tested Welfare Spending, Washington, DC

36/ US Government Spending 2. *Welfare Spending Chart US from FY 1997 to FY 2017,* www.usgovernmentspending.com/welfare_chart_40.html

37/ National Geographic (2007). Hip-hop planet: roots of the music that can't be ignored, Tampa, FL, April 2007 Issue

38/ The Holy Bible, New International Version (1973). Colorado Springs, CO, International Bible Society

ABOUT THE AUTHOR

Richard Siems has a BS degree in Engineering. He worked as an engineer, engineering manager and executive for over twenty-five years in multi-national corporations in the chemical processing industry. He has traveled extensively for both work and ministry. Having been raised in the finest of Christian homes, he was called to inner-city ministry in his early fifties. He ministered in the inner-city full-time more than a decade. In retirement he still volunteers for and advises both local and foreign ministries.

www.ingramcontent.com/pod-product-compliance
Lightning Source LLC
Chambersburg PA
CBHW070539290526
45790CB00002B/563